The Art of Compassion

The Art of Compassion

Supporting Friends Through Dark Times

A. Foeller

The Liminality Press

The Liminality Press

510 West Walnut Street
#552
Columbia, MO 65205

www.liminalitypress.com

ISBN: 979-8-9891640-4-2
ePub ISBN: 979-8-9891640-5-9

First published by The Liminality Press, 2025

Copyright © Alice Marie Foeller, 2025

Book Jacket design: Carolyn Dyess

All rights reserved. No part of this edition may be reproduced, stored electronically or in any retrieval system, or transmitted in any form or by any means electronic, mechanical, photocopied, recorded, or otherwise, without written permission from the Publisher.

Table of Contents

Introduction vii
    You Could Be That Person
    What We Have Been Taught

Chapter 1: Sympathy Seemed Like Something I Thought I Would Like ... 1

Chapter 2: The Last Time Daniel Lay Down on the Couch ... 5

Chapter 3: Early Grief ... 25
    The First Days ... 25
    Anger, Relentless Anger ... 29
    Fear ... 32
    The Fog ... 33
    Everything, Now ... 35
    Live Music, Straight to the Heart ... 37

Chapter 4: Nothing We Did Helped ... 41

Chapter 5: Logistical Nightmares ... 47

Chapter 6: The Stories We Tell About Our Past ... 57

Chapter 7: A Special Brand of Grief ... 65
    A New Grief Model ... 74
    It's "Simple": Don't Be Scared ... 77

Chapter 8: Thoughts on Prevention ... 79

Chapter 9: Ways to Support and Ways Not To, and It's Up to the Bereaved ... 89

Chapter 10: My Declaration ... 99

Chapter 11: Finally, My Grief Exceeds My Anger ... 107

Chapter 12: It's Okay to Triumph ... 113

Epilogue: Bringing Others Along ... 119

Introduction

You Could Be That Person

Have you ever noticed when something bad happens, there are a few people who seem to know just what to do, and they calmly busy themselves doing all the right things? They walk straight up to people who have just received terrible news and they stay with them, unflinchingly. They seem unconcerned about saying the wrong thing. They are graceful and calm.

Then there are most of the rest of us, calculating in our heads whether we are close enough to the grieving person to insert ourselves legitimately in the situation. We might be playing out the whole conversation in our head, memorizing things to say: "I'm so sorry for your loss," and "I have no idea what you must be going through."

What if all of us could be that calm, confident friend?

When my spouse took his own life, a few people knew what to do and moved toward me, calmly and with the kind of support I welcomed. I took note, as much as I could at the time, and I was grateful. Some people seemed to know universal truths about holding space for grief that others did not. Here are some of the main supportive behaviors they demonstrated:

- Don't give grieving people extra mental work
- Be neutral
- Be low-maintenance
- Welcome awkwardness, silence, and unpredictable conversation

These simple practices were extremely helpful to me after I discovered my husband's body on that cold January morning.

What We've Been Taught

Most of us learned everything we know about grief from a combination of personal experience and a day or two of high school psychology class, based largely on the five stages of grief as theorized by Elizabeth Kübler-Ross: Denial, Anger, Negotiation, Depression, Acceptance.

The popularization of Kübler-Ross's stages was groundbreaking for its time. It was good to start somewhere, and the five stages at least gave us language to speak about grieving as a process; but we now know Kübler-Ross never meant for her five stages to apply broadly, beyond the terminally ill patients she was studying.

Today we have new research and resources for the bereaved. We have developed new language and an expanded capacity for compassion—both are beginning to catch on. For my part, I find it helpful to focus on three general phases of grief: shock, integration, and recovery.

Shock: This is the initial time after the loss, when the prefrontal cortex is not functioning, and fear and adrenaline are high. It may be difficult to eat or sleep or both. Support is needed right away. The grieving person needs company, someone to handle their responsibilities, care for their children, feed their pets, make meals, and be a gentle listener.

Integration: The fact of the death or trauma becomes more woven into the fabric of life each day. The chores of death are undertaken—disposition of the body, memorial service planning, legal forms, probate court actions. Often many conversations delivering the news are part of this stage, which can be helpful or traumatic or anything in between. Other activities not related to the loss are often a welcome distraction.

Recovery: The person experiencing grief begins to re-engage with life and seek support to return to work, access grief resources, and ultimately come back to loving.

I will provide additional detail about each phase with examples from my experience, and share actions loved ones can take to support someone moving through them, especially the first two. That is the

Introduction

purpose of this book: to spread these kinds of tips and ideas more broadly. There are plenty of resources aimed at grieving people, but precious few to train us how to be good friends and effective supporters.

Not everyone will be able to read this book and achieve a state of Zen around the trauma and grief of others, especially if they haven't moved through it themselves. However, everyone CAN learn some simple guidelines and gain enough understanding of traumatic loss and grief to be comfortable showing up for a friend. Being comfortable wards off fear. That's why I'm willing to share the nasty and unvarnished realities of my inner experience during this time of surviving my partner's suicide. Everyone's experience won't be like mine (in fact few will), but by pulling back the curtain, I can dissolve the mystery and fear that keep good friends from being the kind of supporters they truly want to be.

Having lived through traumatic loss, I know that people in the early days of grief are in shock and rarely have the capacity for reading or taking in much information. In fact, people experiencing grief or trauma are often living in a strange space somewhere between the familiar past and the unrecognizable and uninhabitable present. They are in a state of "being in between," or liminal space, that makes it unlikely they will want to read books or actively learn something novel in addition to all the unwelcome newness they are stumbling over daily. The rest of us are responsible for walking them through their journey.

If someone is stuck in grief, unable to move forward or return to living, he or she often depends on loved ones to make the difference. All of us around the outside must learn how to do better at supporting the grieving process—and preferably learn about grief before the knowledge is needed. In fact, let's create a groundswell of friends and family who are confident and unafraid to really show up powerfully in someone's time of loss, shock, and sadness.

Think of this book as a graduate course in being a good friend to someone who is going through tragedy or loss. You'll have that degree in hand next time crisis rears its head. Or at least you'll feel confident picking up the phone or knocking on the door. Armed with this knowledge, you aren't going to be the person dropping off dinner on the porch and running away.

Chapter 1

Sympathy Seemed Like Something I Thought I Would Like

> *There is a crack in everything. That's how the light gets in.*
>
> - Leonard Cohen, *Anthem*

I was much younger than my brother and sisters. When I was a little girl, I was always trying to get them to notice me and include me, despite being too little to keep up with them. As I grew older, I was a quirky kid who didn't have a lot of friends at school. I craved attention, but I was often left out. When I read a children's book about a girl named Madeline getting appendicitis and all her schoolmates coming to the hospital to visit her, I was envious. I fantasized about coming down with some terrible illness so everyone would come visit me and notice me.

These days, as an adult, I have a more polite way of describing my desire for attention. Fans of *The Five Love Languages* book (Gary Chapman), refer to it gently as a request for "Quality Time." But if I'm honest, I'm still the same little girl wanting to be noticed.

Since I used to dream of having something bad happen so that people would pay attention to me, I was quite surprised at how it felt to experience something bad and have everyone give me sympathy. It was not at all how I imagined it would be.

The attention turned out to be complicated.

The sympathy turned out to be too seductive; it was incredibly tempting to take a pass on everything, forever.

***

I was 46 when I finally got to experience something bad enough to warrant the sympathy I had fantasized about. My second husband took his own life after a battle with depression and a series of adverse circumstances, and I found his body the morning after he drank a bottle of poison.

At that moment, I stepped through a psychological doorway into a period of life that was jarring, painful, and unfamiliar. I felt emotionally alone, except when I found another rare person who had been on the "survived by" list of someone who died by suicide. I was adrift on a sea of financial, legal, and logistical complications, and suddenly without the paddle of my formerly dependable intellect. My brain was stalled but kept trying to fire, like a car engine on a frigid day, and it was terrifying.

I was cold and jittery almost all the time. I wore a winter coat indoors and kept a fidget toy in my pocket.

My heart closed.

My body was in an adrenaline-fueled state of overdrive.

I became instantly angry over the slightest paperwork issue or the smallest incident of ill-mannered driving.

People did pay attention, just like in the children's book:

They brought me dinner.

They clicked the "Care" emoji on my Facebook posts.

They asked what they could do to help.

But it wasn't always comforting.

I came to realize that most people were too afraid of my anger to get close enough to express interest in the details of my sorrow. The self-pity I could generate with or without others was a tempting swamp of sinking expectations.

"I can't do sales anymore."

"My brain isn't working right."

"I'm scared all the time."

It went on and on and was easy to reinforce.

Having a spouse commit suicide felt like a personal betrayal. He had promised to love me and support me in my endeavors. It felt like a breakup, complete with the anguish and disappointment, only permanent. Breakups often come with some hope of eventually reconciling, or reconnecting in the future when circumstances change or hearts evolve. But this rejection was forever.

As an analytical person, I remember a lot of what worked and didn't work to support my grieving process—both from myself and from other people. Although I endured a period of brain fog, it didn't last long; I knew what was happening inside and outside.

As a result of noticing and learning from my experience, I've developed an accidental superpower of listening to others who are grieving or have experienced a traumatic event. I frequently arrive for what I think is a business meeting, only to have my business client unveil their deepest, darkest secret, with no prompting from me. I am now an unwitting force that brings forth authenticity. And I have become a great listener for their vulnerable revelations.

I've also seen the results of being intentional about healing. We live in a world that makes it very easy to give up. We can always find a label somewhere that we can apply to ourselves so that we can just step off the ride permanently and let life roll on by. By taking an athlete's view of physical injury and transferring it to emotional injury, I knew that I might never be the same, but I could emerge stronger if I kept up an alternating cycle of effort and rest until I found something that worked. I knew my humanity and my spirit were meant to heal and grow stronger. I knew that, just as bones grow denser around a fracture, I would eventually have a heart that could love again with a strength that would overpower the scars.

Grieving with intentionality is not an easy road. The easy path is to be passive and remain stuck in it. But there's a much better life, a richer life full of joy and love at the end of the harder road.

I'll never know if I would have shed the whole layer of materialism that I had unwittingly adopted over the years if not for having so many things stripped away.

I'll never know if I would have opened my heart again if I hadn't invited myself to try on love in new forms.

I did know that if grief is a journey through the wilderness, I'd need to keep moving.

And I'm still moving. I've got shit to do.

**

Rumi told us that the wound is the place where the light can enter ... Marcus Aurelius told us that the impediment to action advances action, that what stands in the way becomes the way.

Elisabeth Kübler-Ross told us that the most beautiful people we have known are those "who have known defeat, known suffering, known struggle, known loss, and have found their way out of the depths. These persons have an appreciation, a sensitivity, and an understanding of life that fills them with compassion, gentleness, and a deep loving concern." That "beautiful people do not just happen."

To heal is not to arrive at a place where we are absolved of that difficulty, but where we no longer interpret the presence of it as our finality, our ending.

In a world where most of us die before we are dead, where most of us hyper-fixate on what we cannot control and leave to ruins everything that we can, where most of us fear our humanness and our vulnerability—I hope you find the courage to try. I hope you will come to see that just maybe, beneath the journey you fear to take is the life you had been waiting for, all along.

- Brianna West, *The Life That's Waiting*

Chapter 2

The Last Time Daniel Lay Down on the Couch

> *And when no hope was left in sight on that starry, starry night*
> *You took your life, as lovers often do*
> *But I could have told you, Vincent*
> *This world was never meant for one as beautiful as you.*
>
> - Don McLean, *Vincent*

We had an argument on Friday night, born of Daniel's deep depression and my exhaustion from supporting him through it. He had been laid off from his job (along with more than 1.5 million highly skilled IT workers that month). He had put a lot of hours and stress into learning this job, hoping the stress would ease up very soon. It did, but not in the way he imagined. The layoff was a huge blow for someone who identified with his job as his primary source of self-confidence.

On top of that, I was worn out from being a caregiver for Daniel, who alternated between abject terror and repetitive cycles of hopeless rumination. It had been an eventful year for Daniel. His sensitive spirit had been bombarded by a number of trials and tribulations. He responded to each with outsized anxiety and panic. Through each one, I was holding him while he rocked back and forth on the couch, wailing in psychological agony.

By the time of the job layoff, Daniel's innate kindness and love of beauty were fading in the rearview mirror. Front and center was his growing weariness of life, of aging, of political divisiveness, of global decline. For my part, I was already growing resentful of the time I was spending on comforting him when I would rather have celebrated the good things in life or worked with him to overcome obstacles.

Instead of us treasuring our blessings together, I was there on the couch next to him, keeping him company in his depression and anxiety.

I was there on the couch when I would rather have been with my kids.

I was there on the couch when I would rather have been alone.

And that's how it came to be that, after many months of spending our precious adult time either with my consoling him or with him drinking himself into artificial cheerfulness, I decided to take a day off from "depression support crew." Daniel had told me in the past that he didn't appreciate it when people minimized his feelings or said he was overreacting, but he did understand that sometimes people needed to go recharge themselves after being around him when he was depressed.

It was my weekend with my kids, and I had planned something fun with them. A new friend of mine had invited the kids and me to hike his privately-owned wild forest, and it sounded like the perfect antidote to sitting next to Daniel on the couch, listening to him go over the circumstances of his layoff (again and again), and his version of his prospects for the future, which were bleak. Of course, they weren't bleak from my view, but he could only see from his, and he repeatedly dismissed my ideas and reassurances that we would get through it together.

I told him I was going to go away on the hiking trip Saturday to get some respite and be with my kids, and then I'd come back and spend time with him Sunday.

He picked a fight with me.

He was jealous. He was upset I would do a family activity with a friend, especially a guy.

Friday night before I left, I said, "Love, we'll work through this like we always do." He looked at me sadly and said, "I just don't know if I want to work through this one." He wasn't sure he had it in him. He didn't want to learn another job; he didn't want to work through a relationship issue with me. He was in despair.

Suddenly he switched from despairing to cold. His eyes narrowed and he told me to leave. It was his house, even though I lived there half the time.

"Go. Just go," he growled, his eyes piercing mine.

I had a rule that I don't stay where I'm not wanted.

"I'll leave, but I'm not leaving you," I said softly. "I'll be back."

I drove the short four miles to the house I have with my kids. When I was getting ready for bed alone in my bedroom, I texted Daniel from my iPhone. He has an iPhone too, which means our text messages always show up with a blue background. But this time my text message turned green. Had he blocked my number? The very idea flooded me with anger. And worry. He had never blocked me, not in nine years. I texted once more, but my message was again green instead of blue.

    I called. Immediately the call went to voice mail. I was irritated and concerned, but also a little relieved. I had already been over all of his worries and fears with him a hundred times a day and there was nothing more to say. I was going on a day trip the next day to get a break from caretaking. Sure, I could spend an hour trying to reach him or driving back over there, but he already told me to leave, and I didn't really want to re-engage in the drama at 11:30 at night.

    I wanted to go to sleep. So, I went to sleep.

The next morning, I headed out of town with my older son, who was excited to go hiking. My younger son had decided to stay near home and spend time with his girlfriend.

    I thought of Daniel all morning, but the way he spoke to me Friday night, I felt like he had broken up with me. Although I didn't accept the idea of breaking up, I wasn't yet ready to dig in and repair it, and I also didn't feel welcome in his life at the moment. Every time I thought about reaching out, I remembered he had blocked me and told me to leave. I figured that I ought to respect his wishes and give him some space.

    By mid-day on that cloudy Saturday, my son Noah, my friend, and I were deep into the pristine forest. It wasn't extremely remote, like Montana, but there weren't any cleared paths and there was no cell service. After a lot of hiking, I found myself at the top of a tall hill in a clearing. After a few hours in nature, I had softened again toward Daniel. He had spoken angrily last night, but he was under a lot of stress. I was worried about him. He'd been anxious and depressed for our whole nine years together, but never as thoroughly defeated by it as he'd been for the past year. He had sometimes spoken of suicide, and that fear wasn't far from my mind all morning. I pulled out my phone to see if I could get service, and up there on the hill I could. I immediately called Daniel's cell phone and it went straight to voice mail again. I asked his next-door neighbor to text him and see if her messages would go through. She said hers were green (undelivered) as well.

Pacing on the hilltop in the January wind, I went up one level in emergency protocol and dialed Daniel's house phone.

He answered, surprised.

Relief flooded through my body. He was still alive. My relief was short-lived, though.

His voice sounded drunk or drugged and maybe just very sad. He said, "I thought you were going to be gone all day." I said I was, but I reached the top of a hill and had phone service for a minute, so I wanted to try to reach him because I was worried about why my calls and texts weren't going through. He denied blocking me and said that something had gone wrong with his phone, and that other people were also reporting their messages not going through. This explanation sounded fishy to me. An information technology security professional, Daniel ran every phone update promptly and hoarded extra charging cables.

But that wasn't as suspicious as what he said next. He told me he had work to do around the house because someone had gotten inside the house and had made a mess and moved things around.

His claim was very hard to believe. Daniel was a stickler for home security, with video doorbells, redundant alarm systems, a panic button, and a safe full of guns. The notion of someone getting into the house while he was there and ransacking the place was laughable, if not downright impossible. I didn't believe him, but he almost never lied to me, so it was very concerning that he would tell me this story.

The hand that was holding my phone was getting very cold in the winter weather. I stuffed my free hand farther into my coat pocket. I said, "You don't sound well." I asked if he'd taken anything that might be making him sound strange.

"I haven't had any alcohol to drink, and I didn't eat or drink anything that might have been spoiled," he said. This was a very clinical answer, even for Daniel, who was often overly literal. I knew I should press him a little because he obviously was avoiding telling me something.

I tried again, "Well, you just don't sound right."

"It's been a hard year," he said slowly, in a low voice.

I said I had to go, because my hiking party was heading out and I didn't know where I was if I got separated from them. I told him I loved him. He said, "I love you, too," sounding almost surprised about that. We said goodbye and I hung up.

I bounded down the hill to reach the other two, but a cold fear gripped my heart. After years of listening to him talk about suicide, and how he would do it, and why his past attempts didn't work, this was the closest I'd been to thinking his ideations might become reality. But I was miles away, even from the car, and a couple of hours away from him.

The shameful part was that I didn't feel drawn to fix it in that moment. If that's what he was contemplating, I wasn't sure I wanted to interrupt it. It sounds cold, but he was so miserable, and I felt it futile to keep trying to pull him out of a miles-wide depression. If he was waiting for me to leave so he could carry out his plan, maybe it was best that I stay away.

Sometimes I hear of situations where a suicide was interrupted and everything worked out, because that person finally got the support they didn't know how to ask for. Their suicide attempt was a call for help, and the person who found them in time was shocked to know that something was seriously wrong. They were propelled to action. The situation was taken seriously where it may not have been before.

This was not that kind of situation. Daniel was neither young nor impulsive. He was about to turn 52. He had been clearly communicating that he wasn't able to cope with recent adversity. He was not hiding it from me. He was not hiding it from his friends. He was on the phone a lot, telling people how hard everything was. He had the tools to pull himself out of it, and he wasn't using them. It was his own mind creating the trouble, and only he could turn that around. He wasn't taking any advice from me. He refused to admit that things could get better. His mind was churning through dark, distorted thoughts, and he was only becoming more tired and filled with despair.

After the hike, my friend and son and I went to dinner in the town nearby, and I sent Daniel a text with a screenshot of my earlier messages. "I sent these earlier, but I don't think you got them," I wrote.

"A lot of messages are sent double to me today. Not just you," he replied. But he didn't address the substance of my messages, which said that I loved him and wanted to keep working on our relationship and supporting him. I just needed a short break for the day, but also, I was seriously worried about him.

That night, I returned home with my son and got ready for bed, still filled with a mix of dread and anger.

"Hi, we are home now," I wrote, sitting on the edge of my bed. "Would you like any help with cleaning up at the house?"

"No thank you," he wrote back simply. Coldly, I thought.

I tried again. "Yesterday you told me to leave, so I want to continue to give you space if you want it. But also please know I want to see you and I'm available to you now and tomorrow," I persisted.

"I understand. I'm going to bed now," he replied.

"Okay," I wrote. "Rest well."

Later I would realize he did not write, "I'm going to sleep now." He very specifically just said he was going to bed.

In the morning when I woke up, I sent him a text. "Good morning, Love. I was planning to spend the morning with you. Do you want to see me?" I offered. "May I call?" The iPhone promptly marked my message as "not delivered." I pulled on my clothes, and called to the kids through their closed bedroom doors that I was heading over to check on Daniel because I didn't think he was feeling well.

On the way over, I sent a message to his neighbor Linda, saying I was worried about Daniel and coming over to check on him. When I pulled into the garage, I sent her another note: "I'm in the garage." She wrote back that I didn't need to give her a play-by-play, just let her know he was okay.

As soon as I put my hand on the doorknob, I had the sense he was not going to be okay. I keyed in the door code and opened the door.

It was quiet.

"Love? Daniel?"

My heart beat faster. The house felt cold.

I took off my shoes quickly in the laundry room as he always required. I walked into the kitchen. I could see into the TV room through the doorway. That's where he often was, lying on the couch watching TV, or sleeping. As I moved quickly, the end of the couch came into view through the doorway, and I could see his head at the end of the couch in its usual position. One part of my brain said, "See, there he is!" but the other part said, "He didn't answer you."

And he wasn't moving.

Blood roared in my ears.

I sped up as I came into the TV room, up to the back of his

head. I had enough time to take in the sight of a plastic lunch cooler beside the table, plus his usual array of things on the coffee table—his watch, his earring, and his phone—before I came around the end of the couch so I could see him.

His hat was pulled down over his eyes. His body was motionless. And his sweatshirt sleeve was pulled halfway up his forearm, exposing a few inches of skin, which was very obviously not right. His flesh was bluish and dull.

That was the end of all hope, right then. There was no chance he was just sleeping. Or that he had taken some drug but was still alive.

No.
This was it.
Dead.
Cold.

A bit rubbery when I touched him.

I was panicky right away, even though there was nothing to be done. Unlike the essays I've read about being at a deathbed, being calm and still as they pass and honoring their spirit, this was alarming, angering, and

just

so

final.

My heart was hammering, my pulse pounding in my ears. My hands were sweaty. My stomach was an empty hole. Everything was pointless and hopeless, and the man who could comfort me when I felt scared was never going to answer me, ever again.

I had been straining to do more, to support him, to balance that with my own needs, to try to figure out the harmony, and then it felt like time stopped. There was no fixing anything. No second chances.

He had crossed the threshold from life to death, and I was crossing one, too. I was lurching from the predictable life I had known into a liminal space that seemed to have no time or measure. Five minutes ago, I was a beleaguered, worried spouse. Now I was a widow. I didn't yet know what that meant.

Grasping for some sense of familiarity in this suddenly new and awful world, I found the "doing" part of my brain still online. I started to calm myself down by trying to figure out how to respond. It was a welcome distraction.

First on the list, I had told Linda I would text back when I knew he was okay. I had not written her back. I called.

"Linda, love, he's not okay. He's dead."

It seemed more real when I said it out loud.

"Nooo!" she wailed. "Do you want me to come over?" Linda had lost her husband to suicide many years before.

"No," I said. "You already had to do this."

"Okay," she said. "Try not to have the police come if you don't have to."

"Yeah, good idea," I said, and hung up.

A note. He probably left a note. It was likely one he had drafted many times before.

I found no note on the coffee table. I found nothing in the kitchen. I tore through the house, up the stairs. Nothing on the bed, nothing in his office. I stuck my head into my own office and saw a manila folder on the chair where I work. I ran to it and saw Daniel's crooked handwriting.

"Will/Death Docs" was written on the label. And on top was a post-it that said, "Note is in Pages app on my phone."

I ran back downstairs to his phone and keyed in the password to unlock it. I opened the Notes app. There was only one note:

> To whom it concerns:
> All of my passwords, including laptop BIOS, Windows, gun safe, house alarm, etc. are in the 1Password utility on this phone. Its password is: E3tE
> My end-of-life documents originals are in my safe deposit box, number 157, at Huntington Bank, 630 South State St., Westerville, OH 43081. The keys are in my gun safe. Copies are in my normal household files under "will/death docs".
> Per my Will and previous discussions with Alice M. Foeller, she's the executrix, sole beneficiary, and sole administrator of my estate. Alice's judgement and wishes

are final, that's why I made her executrix, sole beneficiary, and sole administrator.

Alice can easily spend just a few hours going through the house to find and collect my very most personal things, especially my laptops and external drives, and then simply outsource the rest of the estate duties as desired so that she doesn't have to spend a lot of time on any of this.

Why? This isn't anyone's fault, no one is to blame, and no one could have done anything to help. I'm desperately tired of living in a world that doesn't even remotely share my values or focus, and I also believe there is absolutely no point or higher purpose in life or existence. Additionally, my future feels increasingly bleak with diminishing hope of improvement (depression, anxiety, reclusion, aging, boredom, frustration, futility).

Please disclose the cause of my death and these exact reasons freely to whomever wants to know, I don't want there to be any confusion or misunderstanding in anyone's mind as to why I did this.

- Daniel

Reminders:
- include 1Password above
- reboot phone so it requires local password, which only Alice has
- "Note is in 'pages' app" on phone screen
- turn off furnace
- use the toilet
- remove any desired texts/voicemails

That was the note.

Practical to a fault, he had already turned down the thermostat before he died. Those reminders were to himself, he just forgot to delete them.

I'm including the note here because some of it was incorrect, including the password he left, and it's a good reminder that he wasn't in his right mind during the final hours. I mean, of course he wasn't, but it's comforting to me to see that he wasn't functioning on a practical level either.

The detailed page I found in the file folder about being an organ donor made me especially angry. "Look asshole," I said, out loud, "If you want to donate your organs, you must die at a hospital! And you can't poison yourself!"

There was a separate document in the folder about his burial wishes, which I already knew about. He wanted to be cremated. He definitely didn't want to be embalmed. And he wanted a party instead of a funeral. He wanted people to be self-expressive and dress sexily if they wanted to, and have it feel chic with a Japanese minimalist theme.

He had thought about it, thoroughly, for years. Anytime we went to a funeral home for a relative of mine, he would tell me how much he hated funeral homes and would describe the party he wanted to have.

I read through all his notes and documents.

I stood in the kitchen behind a wooden chair with his red Carhartt jacket slung over the back. I had bought him that jacket. It was hard to find a red one, but the red one he was wearing in 2014 when he first took my hand and put it in his pocket against the cold developed a broken zipper, and I was sentimental about replacing it. I scoured the internet to find the right one, and he had appreciated it. Now in the kitchen, I was cold and sad and alone, and I put the bulky red canvas jacket on over my lightweight black fleece coat. It felt comforting around my shoulders.

I read the suicide note again, and then became more aware of being alone in the house with his body. I figured there was something I should do about that, but I also had the sense that once I called someone, I wouldn't have any peace. I felt the ominous pressure of impending chaos.

As it happened, my hiking trip friend was once a funeral director in a previous turn on his long and winding career path. I had shared with him yesterday that I was worried about Daniel. I called him.

"I found Daniel dead. He killed himself," I said, pausing as I took in the sound of myself saying it. "I'm calling you because I need practical advice. Do I call the funeral home? If I call the funeral home first, can I avoid calling the police?"

My friend's voice was level and calming, after the initial, "Oh my god."

"Okay, the first thing you probably want to do is turn down the heat and crack some windows, depending how long he's been there. And you can call the funeral home first, but they are going to tell you that yes, you have to call the police in a situation like this." He also asked if I had authority to be in the house, and if there was anything of mine in the house that I needed and should remove now. I was confused because I lived here half the time. I said that his note named me the executrix of the estate and the sole beneficiary. He said there were plenty of cases where family members contested the will and people were locked out of houses, and I should be aware of that. I didn't think that was going to happen, but I committed to calling Daniel's sister, the only living member of his immediate family, because she deserved to know right away.

I filed away the information about not having authority to be in the house. It was a disturbing thought, but not one that I thought would be an immediate issue. I thanked my friend and hung up.

I waited to call the funeral home and police so I could hold on just a bit longer to the weird, uneasy peace I currently had. It was like the house was holding its breath. With Daniel there, physically present but not breathing, the usually quiet house felt unnaturally still.

I called Daniel's sister. I told her I had some bad news, and asked if she was ready to hear it. She was driving and she pulled over. I didn't realize it, but this was only the second of many, many calls like this. Kathleen also cried out, "No!" Then we commiserated and she shared about how often she had been talking to him about his job loss and encouraging him. I told her I knew, and that I could tell it made a difference to him when they talked. I told her we had both done the best we could to support him, but it just wasn't enough.

She told me they had spoken the previous day, and he said he was going to meet a friend for pizza. Internally, I scoffed at that idea, but I told her I didn't know, that I had been out of town that evening. I had seen from my phone the prior evening that he set the house alarm, left, drove to an unusual neighborhood for him, and then came home later. There was a box with leftover pizza in the unheated sunroom, but I assumed it was his "last meal" and he ate alone, and then lied to his sister about going out with a friend.

I said I had a funeral home in mind, and asked her if that was okay with her, and that Daniel had wanted to be cremated. She said there was a family plot at the cemetery with her parents, and she could check into that, but yes, it was fine for me to go ahead.

It was unsettling, pacing around the kitchen on the phone with Daniel's body in the next room. But I listened to his sister for as long as she wanted to talk, staying as calm as I could. I answered her questions and recounted how he was handling the job layoff and everything else. Finally, she was ready to say goodbye. I told her I'd stay in touch and coordinate things with her.

The feeling of unease and acute awareness of the body in the next room helped me realize I had limited time. I wanted to do something reverent, something alone, but Daniel was a fierce atheist, and it felt dishonorable to pray over him. I called our close friend and relationship coach, Jessica. She knew Daniel's struggles and anxieties well.

I asked her advice about a way to symbolically say goodbye. She suggested burning sage and perhaps considering some burial rite of a warrior, perhaps from the Norse tradition or the Japanese, sending him on his way. Yes, that felt right. Not to bury him with a weapon, but to acknowledge his passing and honor him in that tradition. I took a bundle of sage from my drawer upstairs and lit it, passing the smoke over his body and the couch, and wishing him well in his forever peace, or at least the end of his suffering and struggling.

I put my hand on his chest.

It was bereft of life.

It felt disturbing. In the place where I'd nestled my head hundreds of times, there was no heartbeat, no breathing, no warmth.

Then I thought about who else might want to say goodbye in person. My kids.

My younger son, Michael, 16, was attached to his phone at all times. The older one, Noah, 18, barely ever answers. So, I called Michael first. He picked up right away. I said, "I have something I need to tell both of you. Can you go into Noah's room and wake him up and put me on speaker?" There was some shuffling and the sound of bedroom doors and Michael talking to Noah and then, "Okay, we're ready."

"Mr. Daniel committed suicide. I found him here when I came over," I said, using the form of address he had requested of my kids when they were younger. I was trying to say the news gently, but it came out flat. I heard gasps and a strangled, "What? No!"

I continued, "Now look, I think dead bodies are weird, and I think YOU probably think dead bodies are weird. I do not want you to come over here as a favor to me. But he wanted to be cremated so if it would help you to see the body and say goodbye, there's limited time to do that and you can come over this morning. But do not come over if you don't want to. There's nothing messy. He took some medicine and just looks like he went to sleep." Michael, the younger one, said he wanted to come. Noah said he would rather not. I said I respected both of their choices.

I gave Michael about ten minutes to drive over and called the funeral home in the meantime. Funeral homes have wonderful, calm, gracious people who always answer the phone, even on snowy Saturday mornings. Someone picked up and I told them what happened. I said Daniel was very clear that he wanted to be cremated and not embalmed. They said that was fine, not to worry, but that I would need to call the police in this kind of situation. They also asked if I was the next of kin and I said yes, I was Daniel's legal domestic partner and he said in his note that all of the decisions were up to me. "Oh, he left a note," said the person on the other end of the line. "Good, that will help things." I hadn't thought about how it might be if he hadn't. Later in a support group for survivors of suicide grief, I met people who hadn't gotten a note, and I am now very grateful for the one Daniel left.

I hung up and called the Blendon Township Police non-emergency line. I said that I had arrived here this morning and found my life partner dead on the couch, and that he had committed suicide. They said they would send someone right away. Remembering what Linda asked, I said, "Please don't use the sirens if you don't have to. He probably died last night. There's no rush."

Michael arrived just as I hung up, and came in through the garage, carefully removing his shoes as always. We had a long, teary hug and I took him into the TV room and said he didn't need to do anything specific, and that I could leave him alone if he wanted. He said he didn't need that, so I stayed. He walked up to Daniel's body, crying quietly, and stood there for a few minutes. We were interrupted by the sound of sirens approaching.

An officer came in through the garage and didn't remove his shoes. He said he was sorry for my loss, and that he wasn't from Blendon Township because they were running behind with the snow on the roads, but he was the first who could arrive from a neighboring township. I took him into the room with Daniel's body. I noticed he was getting snow on the carpet and cringed. I saw Michael notice, too. I stood near the couch while the officer checked for a pulse, which seemed completely ridiculous to me,

And then I went back to the kitchen to watch for more arrivals as he stood in the doorway, asking me basic questions.

I told him what time I had arrived.

I said no, I wasn't really surprised that this happened. Daniel was depressed and had recently lost his job. Yes, he left a note.

He told me it would be a good idea to move one of the cars from the garage so people could get through more easily and didn't scrape the cars with any equipment. That seemed like a good idea. I noticed the empty police car in the driveway with the lights left flashing as I backed my car out on to the driveway, leaving the way clear.

I had been in the house for a couple of hours by then, and never thought I would lose access to anything, but when I returned from moving the car, I noticed the officer was standing in the doorway of the TV room in a pretty authoritative way. As I moved toward the doorway, he shifted his weight and took up more space.

"Am I not allowed in there anymore?" I asked.

"I'm sorry ma'am, but no. This is considered a crime scene now, technically."

That put me back on my heels, literally and figuratively. "Well, I wasn't ready to…I mean…will I be able to see his body again?" I asked.

"Oh yes, the coroner will come, and they will give you time with the body before they take it away," he assured me. "Okay," I said, and breathed a sigh of relief. I didn't know what was going to happen next, but it would be okay.

I moved awkwardly around the kitchen, looking for something to keep my hands busy. Not knowing when I'd be back here, I started the dishwasher. I turned up the heat from 50 to 68. The officer said we were waiting for paramedics. I found that somewhat insane, but I could tell I was not in charge anymore. More officers showed up and introduced themselves and asked me the same questions.

Paramedics came to confirm that Daniel was dead. The neighbors on the other side texted to see what was wrong over here. I texted back that Daniel had committed suicide. That was when I first began to realize that hardly anyone knows what to say when you tell them that. The words themselves are like a bludgeon. The neighbors wrote that they were very sorry and then wrote nothing else ever again.

A detective arrived from Blendon Township. She was kind.

I periodically checked Daniel's phone on the kitchen table as officers milled around, tracking snow everywhere. I could see through the doorway that they had moved the coffee table from its very particular place on the carpet. It had never moved in the 9.5 years I'd been here. Nothing had ever changed in this house.

It felt awful to see the coffee table dislodged. Daniel would have absolutely hated all of this. Maybe he wouldn't have done it if he would have known they were going to get snow on the carpet, I thought to myself.

The detective asked me all the same questions again. She asked to see the note. As soon as I handed her the phone, she put it in Airplane Mode and turned away from me. I had already texted myself a copy of the note, but now I felt suddenly on edge. Were they going to take the phone? Friends were already texting him and I needed to let them know he was gone. She was reading the note, and then she did not give the phone back.

"I need to have that back," I said. "All of the passwords to everything are in there. The alarm system, the doorbells, the bills…everything."

She looked sympathetic and explained that the phone was now evidence, and they would be bagging it and taking it away. He specifically said in his note to delete his personal things from the phone. I felt caught between my dead partner's final wishes and someone with a badge. She tried to be nice and even offered to type in the password for me. But by now the phone was in airplane mode and I don't know if she typed it correctly or not, but it didn't work. We tried a few more times and the password manager would not open. She was grateful that I knew the password to unlock the phone generally. She said that would help.

It didn't help me. There was no way I would get into his computer, not past the 16-digit passwords he changed periodically. How would I pay the electric bill or the mortgage?

She asked Michael and me to wait in the formal living room for the coroner to arrive. We sat next to each other in stunned silence. I felt vaguely like I was in trouble.

"Who turned the dishwasher on?" someone asked.

"I did," I said.

"What time did you start it?" they asked.

This was getting scary. Did they think I killed him? No, they couldn't. He had left a note.

She asked if I knew what he might have taken to kill himself. I said I found a box of Dramamine in the trash, but that couldn't have done it alone. I remembered he told me about taking Xanax and vodka to fly internationally and someone had told him that he was lucky he woke up on the other end of the flight. I knew he had some Xanax and there was always vodka, but I couldn't find the Xanax or even an empty pill bottle. We went through the trash but found nothing. We were stumped.

I said he might have had something else he kept in reserve, but I had never run across it. I knew he researched that kind of thing, and I remembered him vaguely offering to procure something for a relative who had cancer, in case things got a lot worse for her.

Then the detective said she needed the next of kin to sign for the body to be transferred, and asked if I was next of kin. I said yes. She said, "Were you married?" I said, no, but I was his life partner, and his legal domestic partner registered in the City of Columbus, and the executor and sole beneficiary of the estate.

She said she hadn't heard of that kind of domestic partnership. I insisted it was real and legal. We had a ceremony and everything. I had the certificate upstairs and went to get it. The coroner had arrived by then and both the detective and coroner followed me upstairs. I showed them our framed certificate of domestic partnership, but the detective still looked skeptical.

"I've never come across that before and we have to follow the law, so I'm going to have to go with his sister as being the next of kin for now. If she wants, she can sign her next of kin status over to you," she explained.

I started feeling worried. If I wasn't next of kin, did I even have a right to be in the house? Was I trespassing? I tried to put it out of my mind. Surely, Kathleen would be happy to cooperate and make sure I could get the "chores of death" completed. It would be okay. But my friend's warning resurfaced in my mind. What if this wouldn't be simple and I would have to fight for the house in addition to grieving and planning a memorial?

But there was nothing for me to say but "Okay."

I looked up Kathleen's number and gave it to the detective. I texted her quickly that the detective would be reaching out to her for some formalities because she was next of kin.

They asked to see Daniel's office, and by chance a list of his current medications was on his desk as part of his paperwork for sleep apnea. He was supposed to be getting a CPAP machine. He hated the idea, but I had taken a video of him while asleep and showed him the length of time he would stop breathing. After that, he finally agreed to do something about it. I thought it might be the silver bullet. Maybe his anxiety was due to being chronically sleep-deprived. Now we would never know. Now he had stopped breathing forever. I made a mental note to call the company and make sure they didn't ship a CPAP. We looked around to see if there was anything else useful on his desk, and the coroner took photos of the medical records.

We stopped to talk at the bottom of the stairs when my phone rang. It was a friend of mine, a stout, no-nonsense woman I liked very much. I almost sent it to voice mail, but instead I answered.

"Hey, how's it going?" Sharon asked.

"Actually, pretty terrible. I'm over here at Daniel's house and I found him; he committed suicide last night," I said.

"Oh my god," she said, "do you want me to come over?" It was one of the few times in my life when I didn't consider anyone else's feelings or preferences.

"Yes," I said, "actually, that would be really great. But you don't have to do that, honestly."

"I'm on my way. Kevin will drive me, but he'll be happy staying in the car. Send me the address."

And that was that. At least I would have someone around who wasn't counting on me for anything, accusing me of anything, or maddeningly dead.

Sharon arrived about 10 minutes later. I don't remember her coming in the door, suddenly she was just in the foyer. She is one of those people who confidently knows what to do. When she arrived, I was busy answering the exact same questions for the fourth time, this time with the coroner. The coroner was apologetic about asking all the questions again. The snow had slowed her drive across town and she arrived later than everyone else.

I no longer knew if it was morning or afternoon. I wasn't hungry or thirsty. I wasn't tired or even sad. I was mostly numb, logistically on high alert with a thousand things to do piling up (writing the obituary, calling all of our friends, coming up with the perfect place for the memorial), and vaguely worried about the password situation and the next of kin issue.

Someone told me Kathleen had just given authorization to transport the body.

Great.

Wait, wait…the body.

"Hey, they told me I could have time with him again before you take him," I said to the small, young lady who was the coroner. I guess she was technically an assistant coroner or something. The coroner is an elected official. An elected official I had actually met and respected, I remembered. Maybe I could get this next of kin business sorted out later.

She smiled and said, "Yes, don't worry. They would let me know before they took him."

"But can she see him now?" I heard Sharon's authoritative voice demand.

"Oh, well, they've placed him in the bag already, and once that's zipped, we aren't allowed to unzip it unfortunately." She may have said more than that, but the roar in my ears drowned it out. I moved toward the kitchen and the TV room, and I was filled with rage. They had promised me. They promised me I would see him again. And then they wouldn't let me in the room. I just wanted to see him one more time. I didn't have any warning that the last time would be the utterly final last time.

When I looked into the TV room, I saw a body bag strapped to a gurney. Everything in the room was in the wrong place. The snow had melted on the carpet in dingy, shoe-shaped arcs.

I retreated to the foyer where my son was standing patiently, and Sharon was advocating for me. The uniformed people were sorry, sorry I couldn't see him again. They understood that I was promised, but unfortunately, there was nothing they could do.

More questions.

Was he seeing a therapist? Yes.

Was he taking any meds for depression? No, he didn't want to.

Did he leave the house and meet anyone? Well, he went to a very weird place to have pizza that I had never known him to go, and maybe he was meeting someone to buy a drug or something. I didn't know.

There was a call from the kitchen. The gurney with the black body bag had been moved to the kitchen. The coroner told me to go there now; this was the time I could have a moment.

Really?

Have a moment with a black bag? With a bunch of strangers standing around in the kitchen? With their shoes on?

Still, if time with a black bag was all I could have, I would take it.

I leaned forward and curled onto his body, wanting to be comforted the way I'd been so many times. A sob lurched out of me and then I heaved more and more of them. I felt Michael's hand softly on my back. I thought to myself, it's never okay for a child to have to comfort their parent. I shouldn't have put him in this position. But he's such a good kid. I'm glad he's here.

When I finally straightened up and stepped back, they rolled Daniel out the door.

Chapter 3

Early Grief

That was the thing. You never got used to it, the idea of someone being gone. Just when you think it's reconciled, accepted, someone points it out to you, and it just hits you all over again, that shocking.

- Sarah Dessen, *The Truth About Forever*

The First Days

It's important for me to recount how it felt in those first days after I found Daniel lifeless on the couch. Grief books are usually written long after the author experienced the incident, and often they have forgotten what it was really like. To illustrate with a mundane analogy, when my kids were toddlers, I paid a few dollars for an e-book on potty training. I quickly realized that the parent writing the book no longer had little kids, and that they no longer remembered, nor could reference, the actual experience of teaching a 2-year-old with limited sentience and communication skills, how to control a bodily function. I resolved not to make the same mistake if I ever wrote a book.

I will attempt now, just one year later, to recreate honestly what it was like in the days and weeks after Daniel's death. I will also detail the things that really helped me in these first few days, and the things we can do for anyone in a similar situation.

Every person has a unique experience of grief, and I believe that suicide grief is a special kind. Within suicide grief, there are differences among those suffering the death of their spouse or partner, child, parent, friend, or sibling. And within each of those categories, there are the factors unique to each person and their life history and personality. I don't have a very common personality type, so I'm not sure how many people will be able to relate to many of the responses I had. This is not meant to be a road map, but simply a recounting of my particular thoughts, feelings, and circumstances as I navigated the liminal space between what my world had been and what it would become.

Although my reactions are individual to me, the things that supported me are common to most people who have been through a traumatic or unexpected loss. Most have moved through a period of shock that impacted their ability to function in the short-term. They then moved into a space of integration where the loss shifted from being an outside event that interrupted life to becoming part of life and a part of oneself. Then came the experience of being a healed and whole person again, although one who is never quite the same.

Though the Five Stages of Grief didn't apply well for me, Maslow's hierarchy of needs was a useful model: I first needed my physical needs and safety satisfied before I could process anything or move out of the state of shock.

I wasn't able to sleep the first night.

After I went back home to the kids' house the afternoon of finding Daniel, I called a friend on the phone and then joined a hurriedly convened conference call with a group of friends from a leadership course. We all knew each other very well and it was comforting to share my burden with them. It grew dark while I was pacing around the living room. I'm certain the kids were home, but I can't recall anything while I was on the phone beyond the five-foot radius around my body. My situational awareness was zero.

My sons' father (my ex-husband, David), would return from Florida later that night, but in the meantime he rallied the neighbors and his parents, who came over to my house to visit that evening and sit with me. I remember them coming over, and I remember being grateful that they did, but I'm pretty sure I was stone-faced, almost catatonic.

Even though I was not terribly close to my across-the-street neighbors, it was very reassuring having them in my living room. They moved gently and spoke softly. Later when my boys' paternal grandparents arrived, I felt even more reassured. I was vaguely aware that I was not prepared to handle any requests from my kids. Luckily, they were old enough to feed and transport themselves, but if they had asked something of me, I would not have been in a position to accommodate their request. I didn't feel this temporary abandonment was a crisis because my consciousness was so tightly focused on what felt like survival that I could hardly believe I had children at all. That was another world—one I felt I might return to someday, but not tonight. Having their grandparents in the house allowed me to let go of the guilty piece of me that knew I was abdicating the role of mother. If the kids needed anything, their grandparents were here. Good enough. I could return to inward focus and an endless cycling of thoughts and theories.

David arrived that night. I had my door open, and I was lying in bed, wide awake. I have always been a great sleeper. In times of physical discomfort, in times of great stress, in times of fear, I could always fall asleep. But not that night. I wasn't afraid to go to sleep. I wasn't consumed with thoughts. Sleep simply eluded me. David knocked gently, came in, and sat on the edge of the bed. He was very comforting and shared some confidential things about his personal experience that I remember to this day, which helped me feel better. Then he gave me melatonin supplements and some Nyquil he had picked up on his way over and told me I was really going to need my sleep, so it was okay to take something to help. I did, and I was asleep shortly after. He stayed overnight in his bedroom downstairs as a support to the kids and me, and the next morning brought me a hot breakfast in bed, telling me I needed to eat to keep up my strength. I was enormously grateful.

I learned from this act of kindness the importance of quiet company, which provides a sense of safety. Someone who has experienced something frightening or unexpected can use company, and the company should not expect any hospitality. It is a beautiful gift for a friend to be willing to go to the person who has experienced loss and sit quietly in their presence. And it's best for friends to be prepared to fetch their own glasses of water.

I also learned that in times like this, it's okay to break one's usual rules. For example, I had never, ever taken a sleep aid. And I haven't since. But I'm glad I did that night and the night after. Sleep was critically important.

Nutrition was similarly a priority, and I had neither the ability nor inclination to make food for myself or anyone else. Having David bring hot, good-smelling food to my bedside without asking me first was the only way I would have eaten. If he had asked if I was hungry, I would have said no. If he had asked permission to make something, I would have discouraged him and said it would just go to waste. But the smell of hot food triggered some instinct inside me that was stronger than the despair and horror, and I remembered that food was good and comforting and necessary.

**

One of the first acts of service from someone outside of my immediate family was from my friend Aaron, who went to the Meal Train website and set up a meal train for me and the kids. (This website allows anyone to sign up to provide a meal. The manager of the Meal Train chooses which days are to be covered and provides helpful tips such as favorite restaurants and dietary preferences.)

At first, I felt uncomfortable about using the Meal Train, because I knew I could make dinner if I needed to. But after the first dinner arrived at the door, I noticed relief at not needing to decide what to make: not needing to sort through the available food in the fridge and come up with an end product, not needing to pull together the necessary steps to make a salad, cook a main dish and sides, and have it ready at a time when everyone was home.

There was a fundraising section on the website, and that made me even more uncomfortable. In the end, though, it was almost precisely the amount required for catering and supplies for the memorial, and I was grateful to have it.

On my end, I had posted Daniel's obituary on social media and was flooded with condolences and messages that said, "What can we do?" It was such a relief to paste the Meal Train link, rather than try to think of what people could do.

+++

As I tell my story, I will outline the phases I traveled with action items that helped me and can be helpful to people who are seeking to be supportive.

PHASE: Shock

> ACTION ITEM: Support your loved one to be able to sleep at night and provide hot food that aligns with their dietary preferences whether they ask for it or not. Bring your loved one food that is ready-to-eat. Be prepared for them to refuse it but bring it anyway. Keep trying. Once they are ready to get out of bed, it will be easier if their body is fueled, and they will return to having clarity of thought more quickly if they are nourished.

ACTION ITEM: Go to your loved one and be prepared to sit quietly or talk, and fetch things for them and yourself. At this point, they may not be capable of extending typical hospitality. Make yourself at home and take care of your own needs and theirs.

Anger, Relentless Anger

The people closest to me were doing all the right things. I was being supported well. And yet I was furious.

I always thought anger during grief meant being angry about the death, being angry that the person was gone, being angry at the loss. I experienced a boatload of anger, but hardly any of it felt like it was directly about the loss. My mind was playing tricks by projecting it elsewhere. I was angry at my first attorney, whom I replaced simply because I was so angry. I was angry at Daniel's CPA office, who had the nerve to ask me how he died. (I didn't mind telling people how he died if they had a relationship with me or were friends of Daniel's, but this seemed like indecent curiosity from an office worker.) I was angry at the supermarket, the mechanic, the locksmith. Sometimes I was angry at anything that crossed my path. I was angry at Daniel, to be sure, but I wasn't angry at him for being dead. I was angry with him for making it harder for me to settle his estate. I was angry with him for having too many layers of security.

I am one of those people who has had to train myself to feel the body sensations that go with emotions. As the youngest child of four who was often told to stop crying, stop whining, stop pouting, stop having a tantrum, I learned to tune out my feelings. If I have someone coaching me, and I am concentrating on it, I can experience what worry feels like as it sits like a rock in my belly, and I can feel that suppressed irritation clogs my throat. But in the early days of grief, I didn't have to concentrate at all. I could feel the anger in my body quite clearly. I felt agitated all over. I felt a crawling hatred in my chest. My jaw clenched. I felt fire in my gut. Sometimes a friend would ask how I was feeling and I would say, "I just have so much ANGER in my body!"

I give myself credit for naming the agitation and seeking creative ways to release it. The suicide grief organization in my city mailed me a care package, and it contained a very simple fidget toy: a standard-sized marble encased in a small tube of nylon mesh. If I squeezed one end, the marble squirted down to the other end. I kept it in my pocket most of the time and fussed with it frequently.

The funeral home returned to me the chain Daniel wore constantly around his neck. To be honest, I always hated that chain. When I met him, he wore a thin silver chain and a single earring. It gave him a bit of an outdated punk '90s look, especially when he wore his shirt unbuttoned too far, which he often did. He had nice pecs, it was true! And it was his choice to show them off. But the chain was something I wished he would have outgrown or evolved. Instead, he upgraded to a black stainless-steel chain, which was even more conspicuous, and—being black with large links—looked somehow feminine. I didn't like it from the start. But when it was returned to me in a clinical Ziploc bag, I took it out and put it the pocket of the red Carhartt jacket. It was soothing to play with, piling up the black links into a puddle in my hand, then switching to let the chain flow into my other hand.

I was constantly fidgeting.

Daniel didn't like Christmas, but he bought me a Yule present a few weeks before he died. He paid for sessions with a trainer at his gym, which I had finally joined after years of balking. I went and met with the trainer there, and noticed how vulnerable and exposed I felt when opening my arms or my chest for stretches or exercises. It felt like primal fear. I told her it was a strange sensation, opening my arms wide and experiencing emotional defenselessness. I bore down and did the exercises anyway.

At the second gym session, I asked if there was anything we could do that would help me release anger, like hitting something. Mindy quickly brought me something called a Smash Ball. The exercise is to throw it as hard as possible against the floor. I loved it. I learned to split wood, which took a lot of skill and perhaps more strength than I had but was cathartic.

I remembered everything I could about chakras and tried to be mindful about energy being stuck. When I visited my friend's forest home again, the simple act of returning to the place I had chosen overstaying with Daniel produced so much visceral agitation that I broke through all of my self-consciousness and stood in his kitchen, arms outstretched, asking him to help me move the anger up and out of my throat. I refer to that day as "the exorcism in the kitchen," and it did help, temporarily.

Early Grief

Going through some of Daniel's belongings in the early weeks, I remember finding some things related to one of his friends, whom I wanted to tell what happened. With only a first name and without Daniel's phone, I couldn't reach her. Then I remembered she worked at a tattoo and piercing shop that was owned by someone I had been in touch with regarding a nonprofit youth sports league. At least that guy's contact information was in my phone. I called him to tell him what was going on and asked him to pass along the news. He asked if there was anything he could do. I said, "It's just IN my BODY. I have so much grief and anger in my body. I can't get it out." He said, "Every Wednesday we have a sweat at a local sweat lodge, and it can be very helpful for working through emotions like that." I immediately agreed to attend.

The sweat lodge was unlike anything I'd ever experienced. Contrary to what I imagined, there were no hallucinogens or mind-altering substances of any kind. We arrived in the evening and a large fire built. As it grew in size and heat, the people who were gathered around fed their offerings to it. Then we retreated into a dirt-floor hut covered with animal skins. Red-hot rocks from the fire outside were brought in and placed in the middle of the circle, then water was poured on top, and the animal-skin-door was closed. The experience was one of pitch darkness, searing heat, suffocating steam, and loud, rhythmic, unfamiliar singing and chanting. It was too hot and too loud to think. I could only be present and attempt to keep breathing in air so hot it burned my nose and stung my lungs.

I emerged calmer.

The calm didn't last, but the agitation did ease with time.

+++

PHASES: Shock and Integration

>ACTION ITEM: Be understanding and patient with your loved one's emotions, and help them identify and express their feelings, even in unconventional ways.

>ACTION ITEM: Validate your loved one's feelings. Remind them that whatever they are feeling is okay. Be affirming and curious. This will help them find confidence in exploring their feelings further. It will help them to experience their feelings

instead of avoiding them or stuffing them down to make themselves or others more comfortable.

Fear

I also experienced an acute jumpiness in gatherings of people and stressful situations.

I had signed up to be a guest speaker at my older son's high school journalism class. The date of my presentation was January 27, just five days after I found Daniel at home. By Tuesday, the high school faculty knew what had happened and had mobilized to support my kids. The journalism teacher asked if I wanted to reschedule. I said that I wanted to come and give the presentation because I wanted something else to focus on and I thought the positive energy of the high school class would be good for me.

The day before my presentation, I gathered up some of my journalism awards, old press passes, and a fake front page that my colleagues had printed for me when I left the daily newspaper where I had worked for a few years.

On presentation day, I didn't have trouble concentrating, and I didn't have a problem presenting or even making jokes to the class. But I did notice I was very jumpy, as if on high alert. My startle response in general was highly activated. A loud noise would nearly send me through the ceiling. In traffic, I often thought cars were going to hit me when they weren't even close.

Later, I attended a meeting of women business owners at the group's regular monthly luncheon. When I arrived, several of the women knew what had happened and greeted me in the now-familiar way: eyes opening wide, then a big lowering of mood and energy, a furrowed brow, and "Oh Alice, how ARE you?" I appreciated the concern, but it was hard to fend off the low energy and always be the one to pick it back up. I understand no one is going to approach a grieving widow cheerfully, but I admit it was a burden to pull the mood back up every time. Yes, something terrible had happened, but I didn't want to drag it with me everywhere.

After the meeting began, I was sitting in my chair minding my own business. There were announcements and thanks to the sponsors. I began to look around and worry suddenly that there would be an announcement about me and Daniel, and the entire room would look at me and suddenly emit that pity-energy toward

Early Grief

me all at once.

The idea of it was awful and overwhelming. It was confusing, because at that time, whenever I faced any adversity, I was tempted to shout out that my partner had just killed himself, since I knew that would get me infinite amounts of grace and forgiveness. I did want people to know. But I didn't want that huge rush of sympathy all at once on such a large scale.

I tried to become smaller in my chair. Mercifully, nothing like that happened. It never would have—the group is far too sensitive and caring to do something like that. But the imagined threats were frequent. It felt like life was one big jump-scare movie. I was on edge.

I later learned that feelings of terror often accompany grief, and that even animals seem to experience the same fearful emotions in the same areas of the brain after the death of a family member. The theory is that the feelings of fear push us to seek the company of others when we might otherwise tend to isolate. That's what I was doing.

+++

PHASE: Shock

> ACTION ITEM: Check for fear, trauma, and PTSD-type symptoms in your loved one. While it helped that I wasn't being coddled, I did appreciate being reassured and feeling safe after being on edge all day. I craved hugs during this time, sometimes meeting friends halfway in a parking lot just to be held for a minute.

The Fog

One of the most distressing parts of the early grief experience was lowered cognitive function. I've seen films about people in the early stages of dementia having the experience of losing brain power but still being aware enough to notice it. Suddenly, I knew what that was like. I have always—always—been able to rely on my thinking mind. I can figure things out. I can remember details. I enter appointments in my calendar with 99 percent accuracy. I use spreadsheets with multiple tabs to plan vacations. I took my boys on a 2500-mile tour of 10 college campuses in seven days in an electric are and never ran out of juice. I run a company with nine employees. I've started three nonprofit agencies. I had never gone to the well of my intellect and found it dry, until this point.

I was making mistakes. I couldn't remember conversations. I would schedule a 1pm meeting, remind myself of the 1pm meeting, have a phone reminder set 10 minutes prior, and then call someone at 12:30pm and talk for an hour, blowing straight through the meeting. I went back and forth on decisions 10 or 12 times, including whether to go on the trip to

England and Scotland we had planned. (I ended up not going.) In short, I couldn't rely on myself. That was scarier than anything else I'd encountered.

I stepped back from work a bit, relying on my assistant to handle calls and emails, and relying on my project manager to keep current client work moving. After two weeks, the foggy experience resolved, and I could count on my brain again. I was newly grateful to have something I had always taken for granted, my clarity of thought.

+++

PHASE: Shock

> ACTION ITEM: Be patient if your loved one forgets appointments or commitments or has trouble making decisions. Encourage them to delay on any large decisions that aren't urgent. It's not so much that they will make a poor decision, but more that decision-fatigue is high and what willpower remains must be allocated to "death chores" and urgent legal and financial issues.
>
> If your loved one has a support system such as an assistant, employees, or a family member who helps with work or the household, encourage them to increase their efforts and minimize distractions for the person who is managing a loss.

Everything, Now

One overwhelmingly positive reaction I had was a desire to live, live fully, and do it right now. Why had I not been to the symphony in seven years? Why didn't I go listen to live blues music anymore? Was there a reason I hadn't signed up for that life coaching I wanted to try?

I no longer had a life partner to consider.

I no longer had to temper my zest for life and tone it down so that I could fit into life with a depressed person.

I no longer had to wait until it was convenient for someone else.

Nor did I want to.

Why wait?

Why live small?

Who cares what anyone thinks?

So, in the weeks following Daniel's death, I not only went to a sweat lodge, I also tried psychedelic mushrooms, drove an hour to a tiny bar in a tiny town to listen to blues music, signed up for two kinds of coaching plus hypnotherapy, and drove my motorhome on a one-lane dirt road.

It felt great! And I felt free.

I'm an empathetic person, and part of that great gift is that I can easily sense what will make another person happy. Because I've also often been an insecure person, I then put that person's preference (stated or unstated), ahead of my own.

I was suddenly without a partner and found myself meeting no resistance from anyone. Almost every person I talked to said something like, "You get to feel whatever you are feeling right now. Just do whatever makes you feel better." I had *carte blanche* to live my life. It shouldn't have taken such a tragic event to grant me that feeling, but I felt like I was in college again. Life was a smorgasbord of options, and I could enjoy as many as I could manage.

I was also determined not to have a bunch of favorite places where I felt I couldn't go because they reminded me too much of Daniel. I didn't want our favorite restaurant to be off limits, nor the nature path we frequented. I set about systematically reclaiming these spaces for myself as quickly as possible. I went to dinner alone at True Food Kitchen. I hiked the nature trail by myself.

The last of the "early grief" symptoms related to Daniel's house. I was there alone a fair amount, and it was a nice enough place, but hardly cozy. Daniel never hung any pictures on the walls, and it was a cavernous space for one person. It did feel haunted sometimes. The outside lights, which he was fanatical about, went on the blink—literally. The entire set of lights on the deck started blinking on and off. I got on the phone with a friend of his who helped me troubleshoot, but I ended up just disconnecting all of them to stop the blinking. It really did give me the willies.

I had a friend tell me I shouldn't go there by myself, but in my sudden fit of not caring what anyone thinks, I disregarded that advice. It was my house! I'll go there when I want, I thought to myself. Though I hadn't been in the TV room much—the room where he died.

After an indecently short amount of time, I had a male friend over, romantically. (See above: "do whatever makes you feel better.") I really wanted the comfort of someone to sleep with at night, but it didn't feel right to have someone else in our bed, so we slept in the downstairs bedroom. I told him I wanted to demystify the house. I showed him all around until we came to the TV room and The Couch. I looked at him and he looked at me. He waited and followed my lead. Very gingerly, we both sat down on the couch.

And then it became my couch.

And slowly, week by week, it really did become my house.

And more than a year later, I finally threw out that damn couch.

+++

PHASE: Integration

> ACTION ITEM:: If your loved one suddenly seems fanatical or wants to sell everything and move to Australia, don't be surprised. Support their desire to live life fully while being helpful in not having them lay waste to their career, home, and family. Eventually this stage will run its course, and they will likely want to return to some familiarity, financial stability, and reliable relationships.

Live Music, Straight to the Heart

One of my longest enduring friendships is with someone I met at summer camp when I was 8 years old. Now her late 40s, my friend was getting married for the first time, and she was excited to share in all the associated showers and parties. In the fall before Daniel died, she had been planning a destination bachelorette party in Nashville, Tennessee, and I was excited to be on the guest list. The trip was coming up two months after Daniel's suicide, and just two weeks after Daniel's Memorial. Although the bride-to-be probably felt awkward asking if I still planned to attend, there was no handwringing on my end at all; I was definitely in.

My main concern was that my presence at the weekend would inject a somber note into an event that should be purely celebratory. I didn't have any concern for myself and my ability to handle the weekend-long party. I wanted to get away from everything. I wanted to wear the custom-printed group tank top that proclaimed, "Gettin' Rowdy!" I wanted to drink without worrying about driving home. I wanted to revel. I wanted to prove that Daniel was wrong: life was actually free and joyous.

Members of our group arrived on a few different flights and checked into the hotel throughout the afternoon and evening on Friday. I felt excited. It was so nice to be away from responsibilities and paperwork. The next morning, we all gathered in the lobby for a briefing on our upcoming full day of revelry and fun. I took the opportunity to make a brief announcement. I told the women that maybe they all already knew, or maybe they didn't, but that my life partner of nine years had died by suicide a few weeks ago. And although that's very tragic, I was here for joy and fun. I said that I might get sad now and then, but that I was doing well, had lots of resources I was using to help with my grief, and was focused on enjoying the weekend and being alive. Saying everything out loud was helpful for the group, but I did it mostly for myself. I didn't want it to be the subject of whispers. I didn't want people to think they were supposed to pretend they didn't know. I wanted people to actually check on me and see if I was okay from time to time, rather than casting sidelong glances at me and wondering whether it was alright to ask me.

The weekend was a great success, and there was plenty of laughter, sunshine, good food and stiff drinks.

I went on the trip expecting it would be a distraction from my grief, but I had not anticipated the impact of live music on my emotions. I knew I enjoyed live music, and I had always noticed hearing a song live had more impact than listening to a recording. But watching these talented, soulful musicians in the country music capital of the world playing covers of familiar songs was incredibly emotional. I was pulled into the melodies and the lyrics. The music resonated in me and elicited wave after wave of joy, love, anger, despair, ecstasy, agony, loneliness, and gratitude. With the steady flow of alcohol suppressing my inhibitions, I frequently found myself singing at the top of my lungs with tears pouring down my face. Tucked anonymously into the crowds of dancing strangers, yet knowing a dozen friends were always nearby, I was free to feel deeply and cry loudly.

The low point came Saturday night when I wanted a break from the partying for a bit. A group of us came back to the hotel to retrieve jackets and drop off shopping bags, and I decided I would stay behind and be alone. The moment the door closed behind my friends and I was left in quiet solitude, I started feeling ill with a headache and stomachache. I lay in bed for a while, then decided to go to a nearby drugstore for some ibuprofen and crackers. As soon as I had worked up the energy to leave the room, I realized I had lost my hotel room key somewhere on the streets of Nashville. If I left the room, I wouldn't be able to get back in. The room reservations were not in my name, so I couldn't get a replacement key on my own. My friends had gone back to Music Row.

I waited for some time, fidgeting uncomfortably in bed trying to soothe my head and stomach, which I guessed were reacting more to the strong emotions than any physical illness. Finally, tired of feeling trapped, I texted the bride's sister, also a friend of mine, hoping she would check her phone amid the music and excitement of the nightlife scene. To my great relief, she came immediately to the hotel room with her mother, who was also on the trip. They brought hot tea and a bagel from the snack bar in the lobby, presented me several choices of pain relievers from their purses, and made sure I was comfortable before heading out again. They even managed to get me another room key so I was free to come and go.

During this episode and others like it during early grief, I noticed how deeply I appreciated people who came to my rescue in a moment of need. Throughout my life I've always been grateful for such gestures, but at this time there was an added element of relieved surprise. Overall, I felt as though I was gritting my teeth and pushing through pain daily, so an added difficulty was only a fractional increase in burden. It was almost not worth asking for help. I imagined others saw me as a hiker struggling under the weight of an enormous backpack and were too intimidated to offer help when they noticed a small extra item added to my load. They knew there was nothing they could do to ease the heaviest part of the burden, so they started to avoid even looking at what I was carrying. Or at least that's how it felt to me. Maybe they thought I seemed to be bearing up so well, I must not need any help. But even though my loved ones couldn't relieve me of my grief, having them support me with more mundane issues made me feel safe, loved, and connected. Their actions of compassion interrupted the thoughts in my head that told me I was alone and couldn't count on anyone.

+++

PHASE: Integration

> ACTION ITEM: If you notice a small difficulty you can alleviate or hear a complaint you can resolve, step in confidently and ask to support your grieving loved one with that problem. It's best if you come prepared with a few ideas to solve the issue, and a determination not to be put off by phrases such as, "It's okay, I can handle it." After a major traumatic grief event, your loved one very likely does feel like they can handle a more minor setback, because they are already handling so much else. They certainly can handle this smaller issue. But having support will lead to connection, love, and feelings of safety that aid the broader grief journey. Like my friends at the hotel, come quickly and bring supplies.

Chapter 4

Nothing We Did Helped

> *Killing oneself is, anyway, a misnomer. We don't kill ourselves. We are simply defeated by the long, hard struggle to stay alive. When somebody dies after a long illness, people are apt to say, with a note of approval, "He fought so hard." And they are inclined to think, about a suicide, that no fight was involved, that somebody simply gave up. This is quite wrong.*
>
> \- Sally Brampton, *Shoot the Damn Dog: A Memoir of Depression*

Any good book on grief will delve into the mindset and emotional state of the person who survived, as we are doing here. But with suicide grief, we also delve into the mindset and emotional state of the person who died. Some people become obsessed with how and why the suicide occurred. I can see how that can happen.

Wandering around the house after they took Daniel's body out, it was easy to feel like a detective. Every little scribbled note suddenly carried extra meaning. Everything he owned became a relic or an archaeological clue.

I remember the overwhelming thought, "What is all of this FOR now?" Daniel had a lot of peculiarities, and he purchased a lot of items to deal with his particular routines and peccadilloes. He had huge racks of shelving in the basement to hold original boxes from appliances long gone. He had backups to the backup Wi-Fi router. He had enormous amounts of things he wouldn't throw away.

He operated out of fear quite a bit. (I could recognize it because I did too.) When he would weigh whether or not to lend someone an item, he didn't calculate where that item would do the most good. He weighed how much it would cost him, mentally and emotionally, to not have that item if he suddenly needed it. He was extreme with this behavior. One time, my younger son needed white athletic shorts on a deadline. Michael had just joined the tennis team, they had an away match at another school, and he was told the away uniform required white shorts. He didn't have any. I asked Daniel for advice on where to get men's tennis shorts on two hours' notice. He told me he had some, and lent them to me, but he said he needed them back and I should purchase some for Michael long term.

I couldn't imagine why he would need them back. In the nine years we were together, I had never seen Daniel wear shorts of ANY KIND, much less white athletic shorts with no pockets. It didn't make any sense. But he was convinced that a circumstance existed in the possible trajectories of his life in which he would suddenly need these shorts and be very upset that he didn't have them. This outweighed the fact that the shorts would be put to much greater use by Michael than sitting in a closet for another 10 years; further, Daniel had the resources to purchase new shorts if he needed to, whereas Michael had no money and no driver's license at the time.

The house was full of things like that.

I kept looking around and thought again, "What is this all FOR now? It's all for nothing!"

The handwritten notes he always left around were wrenching because they represented a kind of bankrupt form of hope. There were notes on his desk, on his bedside table. Often, they were lists of things he wanted himself to do more of:

"Meditate."

"Take walks with Alice."

"More time in nature."

But for the most part, he didn't do those things. I was already angry, but it infuriated me to read these lists. He knew what to do to make himself feel better, but he wouldn't do it.

"Dammit, Daniel," one of his friends wrote on the online obituary.

Indeed.

He had a recurring reminder on his phone to ask me about my day. He silenced it daily without asking me. He bought a bicycle that he never rode once. (And a helmet and fancy bike shoes.) He spent a ton of money with an endocrinologist, optimizing all his hormone levels and taking supplements, including supplemental testosterone. (I didn't love the impacts of that, but he insisted it didn't change his personality.) He kept all his possessions in meticulously excellent condition, and that made him feel content, or at least safe. He went for walks outside, up and down the road, as a break from work. In the fall, we rescued wooly bear caterpillars together, scooping them up and carrying them to the other side of the road so they wouldn't get run over. He mounted a big light above his computer monitor, shining in his face, designed to beat the winter blues. If he could've bought happiness, he would have done it.

He had discipline in some ways but lacked the fortitude to get up an hour before work and calm his mind, whether through exercise or stretching or breathwork. He always woke up terrified, just in time to shower, brush his teeth, and face his first appointment.

By the time the memorial service rolled around, a couple of months later, I felt I had a pretty good handle on how and why everything ran off the rails for him.

I summed it up in an essay that I made available for all the people who were shaking their heads and wondering why.

I knew why.

It was no fun having been the person who wasn't surprised, the person who lived with a hopeless, desperate man. But at least I had peace around the "why" question. I felt it was important for me to share, so others could have that same peace.

This was my essay.

***

Listening to him talk about his childhood, I just wanted to scoop up that little boy and hold him, away from his mother, a beautiful woman addicted to prescription drugs, who wrote in her journal, "I never wanted Danny."

I wanted to him protectively against the force of his single-minded father, who was holding the household together and seemed to have the capacity to give approval only in exchange for performance.

But maybe no amount of scooping or holding would have helped, even back then. Who knows.

He overcame a lot of fears and transformed a lot of unhealthy thoughts.

By the time he died at almost 52, he could fly on commercial planes without anxiety meds. He could work (and even sleep), in tall buildings. He believed mothers could love their sons. He believed I could love him. (And I did.)

But just like when you are planning to break up with someone, you don't let in any good thoughts about them; he was planning to break up with life. Some beautiful, kind, loving things happened in those weeks, and he couldn't bring himself to look, lest it hurt too much to turn his back.

He had always been planning to break up with life. His first suicide attempt was just after college, when he moved away from the nature that sustained him, and into a loud, crowded New York City, sharing an apartment with strangers and working at a frustrating job. The second was after a breakup with a beloved girlfriend. Those were the serious ones. There were also the casual discussions of what he wanted at his memorial gathering. The logistical considerations he would share, when he wasn't in crisis, of how to do it in a way that wouldn't leave a mess. The discussions about how I'm so strong, and I would manage to go on with my life. And maybe you are reading this and thinking, "Hey, if he was having suicidal ideations, why didn't you get him help?"

The easy answer is that he WAS getting help. He was seeing a therapist weekly. He was always reading and listening to podcasts, and sometimes enrolled in personal development courses. He refused anxiety and depression medications. (His sexuality was central to his self-image and his ability to receive love and pleasure, and the side effects of those medications would have impacted that in a way he wasn't willing to experiment with.) But he was seeing an endocrinologist and taking supplemental hormones and vitamins to optimize his physical and mental health. He had a CPAP machine on order to help him get better sleep, but it hadn't arrived yet. There was always some magic bullet he was seeking. Maybe just a little more Vitamin D. Maybe a different pillow. Maybe HGH. Maybe micro dosing mushrooms. Maybe the next TED Talk.

The harder answer is that Daniel always told me not to talk people out of suicide. "It's a valid choice," he would say. "If someone wants to check out, they should get to check out." It's just a shame that they must do it in secret because there's no legal way to do it in community with others or holding the hand of a lover. But he also had to do it alone because, like the analogy about breaking up a relationship, he had already chosen this path. If a little love or hope had crept in, it would have only taken more time and struggle to push it out the door so he could turn back to the comfortable, empty, quiet despair.

In the final week, some of the things he said to me were:

I front-loaded a lot of work when I started [my job at] Keyfactor. I worked on my virtual lab every weekend for weeks when I started, to learn the software. And I left there after such a short time, it didn't pay off. And then I did the same thing at Tanium. I worked so hard for months, and it was just going to start paying off, and then I got laid off. I just don't think I can do this one more time.

I just don't know if I want to work through this one.

No matter how much I cry, no matter how many people I hug, no matter how many calls I make I can't get the pain and the fear out. I just want it to stop.

Admit it, wouldn't some part of you be better off without me?

I told him that the layoff was a blessing, and the "golden handcuffs" were off. He wasn't going to find a job like that again anytime soon in this economy with all of the IT layoffs, numbering in the hundreds of thousands. So there. That's gone. Just leave the corporate culture and go do something that makes you happy. I sent him a job listing for a stable hand at the Otterbein University equestrian program. He wouldn't even click on it. "I just don't even see how that would work," he said. I told him he only had to make it for 18 months, until my youngest was off to college and we combined households. I told him I had lived on the cheap for many years and would be quite happy without fancy restaurants. I told him he just had to believe me – believe, dammit – that we were going to grow old together, and this was just a bump in the road.

When we met, Daniel was 43. He shared a playlist of music with me, and all of it was dark, sober…excruciatingly sad. I asked him if he thought he always would be bent toward the sadness. In a moment of optimism, or perhaps just trying to win my affection, he said no. He said he was confident that if he felt safe and loved and had a good outlet for his talents, he could be happy. But he also said, in a different conversation around the same time, that his exit plan was to die (on purpose), in a fiery motorcycle crash at age 45. "I'm not having a great time at this party," he said. So I figure we—you, me, all Daniel's family and friends—got him seven extra years. Or we got ourselves seven extra years of him.

He did see the way we love our children fiercely. He did see the profound beauty in flowers and bugs and dogs and birds. He did see the kindness. We did share his values and his focus. But at the end, when he just didn't have any more left in him, he had to turn away from that so he could find his peace and end the suffering, finally. He had to focus only on the war, the pollution, the injustice, the insecure nature of love, the unstoppable aging of the body, the stumbling economy and the unknown of what might lie ahead. That was the only way he could take an action that would stop the pain.

He told me for years that he woke up every morning feeling terror or dread. I would rib him about his refusal to try exercising in the morning instead of the evening. But in reality, waking up to face the day took an extraordinary act of courage for Daniel, and starting it early seemed unthinkable. But wake up he did, pushing through the dread and rarely taking a day off.

He was brave to wake up every day for almost 52 years. And he was brave to take those pills on the night of January 21st, and tuck himself in with the blanket on the couch (just like he always did), and to take off his glasses, his watch and his earring, (just like he always did), and pull his fleece hat down over his eyes, and go to sleep knowing he wasn't ever going to wake up again.

Don't tell yourself you could have stopped him.

Don't tell me he was selfish.

Don't say it couldn't have been that bad.

This wasn't easy for Daniel. It wasn't easy to live. It wasn't easy to die. It must have been really bad. I knew it was really bad. I walked with him for hours. I held him. I reassured him. I coached him. I looked him straight in the eyes, even when he had tears in his. And for me, with my nice well-adjusted brain and my normal happy upbringing and my natural inborn resilience ... yes, I certainly could have coped with that adversity. I could have gotten up again. I could have worked through it. But Daniel couldn't. And we must forgive him that.

And for heaven's sake, LIVE.
Live your life.
Love as much as you can. Right now.

Chapter 5

Logistical Nightmares

Bitterness is like cancer. It eats upon the host. But anger is like fire. It burns it all clean.

- Maya Angelou, *Conversations with Maya Angelou* (1989)

On top of the physical agitation that flowed from my grief, and in between my nearly manic activities in pursuit of living fully and free, I was attacking my duties as Executor of the estate with zeal.

Because I'm a woman, technically I was the Executrix of the estate. I liked the sound of that. There was something powerful and sort of mystical about being a widow and executrix of the estate. I had a "Black Widow" superhero aura, and I walked around with my jaw clenched and my eyes fiery.

Unfortunately, at the start, all I had was the title. There were no estate tasks I could actually complete. As the country song goes, "All hat, no cattle."

Suicide had its peculiar challenges, one of which was that the perpetrator was dead, but it was still a "crime," in that a suicide is a homicide until it is ruled a suicide. The police were just doing their jobs.

I tried to be understanding. My boys' father had been a police officer for a few years. There are rules and procedures. But it's rough being a survivor of someone who took their own life and having to navigate police processes and investigations on top of everything else. I heard later from my support group that the police often take the suicide note. I'm not sure why I had the presence of mind to text Daniel's note to myself before the police arrived, but I'm very glad I did. It was weeks before they returned his phone to me. For quite a while, I thought I'd never get it back, and I was trying to do everything there was to do with no access to any of the online accounts.

To add to the frustration, the password he included in his suicide note was wrong. Without the password manager, I could not open the gun safe to retrieve the items he had instructed me to find.

***

Monday morning after Daniel died, I started off fresh and contacted the attorney who had drawn up Daniel's will. He was a friend of mine. I had a copy of the will but couldn't file in probate without the original. No problem, I thought. Jack will know what to do.

"Hello, this is Jack," came the familiar voice through the phone.

"Hey Jack," I said. "I have some bad news. Daniel passed away Saturday night and I need your help with his will."

"He couldn't have! I had pizza with him Saturday night!" he exclaimed.

"What?" I said, flabbergasted.

"Yeah, we met up for pizza," Jack said. "We had it planned a couple weeks before and I had a terrible time getting a hold of him. How did he die?"

"He killed himself," I said flatly.

"Lord, have mercy," said Jack.

Jack and I met for coffee the next day because I wanted to know more about how he was acting that night, and because there was something significant and meaningful about meeting someone who had been the last person to see him alive.

The coffee meeting didn't solve any mysteries, but it did give me a chance to lay out the difficulties of obtaining the original copy of the will. The original is required for an estate to be opened, to obtain a bank account for that estate, and to begin the required paperwork. But the original of the will was locked in a safe deposit box at the bank, even though that's something attorneys will expressly say NOT to do. It would have been understandable if the safe deposit box contained some rare coins or something in addition, but it seemed Daniel was paying for the safe deposit box solely to store documents that are best not kept there. Even if I had been able to get the key from the gun safe, they wouldn't have opened the safe deposit box for me, because my name was not on it.

As it was, my attorney had to file a preliminary motion in the probate court to allow him to meet a locksmith at the bank to drill into the safe deposit box and retrieve the will. Meanwhile, I didn't know how much the house bills were, nor if they were set up to be paid automatically. Over time, I learned they were not set for autopay, but that there were phone numbers I could call to pay bills even though I had no access to the accounts. I went through paper files to find the account numbers, then called the phone number for the electric company, gas company, trash pickup, internet, and even the mortgage. Not one of them had any problem taking my money as long as I punched the bank account number into the phone. *My* bank account number.

I never realized how expensive death is. The funeral home was fair, but not cheap. There's no life insurance if you kill yourself, unless you've been on the policy for more than two years, which he hadn't. The attorney I hired ended up being a godsend, but he didn't work for free. In the third month, after I had a death certificate and a checking account for the estate that contained the money Daniel had in the bank, things were a little better. But my attorney advised me that, while I could pay the house bills out of the estate checking account, I couldn't yet take money from that account to reimburse myself for what I spent two months prior when paying the funeral home, the expenses of the memorial party, and the mortgage.

One of Daniel's small Roth IRAs named me as the beneficiary, so I cashed it out and took the hit on the tax penalty. I needed the funds to keep up.

The cause of death in a suicide like Daniel's takes a while to be finalized. Obviously, he ingested something on purpose, and it caused him to die. But coroners don't care about "obviously." They need proof.

In my case, I was waiting on the autopsy mostly for my own peace of mind, and I didn't even realize I wouldn't be notified when the autopsy report was complete. I was still not listed as next of kin, and Daniel's sister had stopped speaking to me. (Maybe she was handling her grief by avoiding as much of it as possible.) I learned about the autopsy report when one of Daniel's other relatives sent me a message to say his sister felt more peace once she read the details of what he had used to die.

I replied calmly, "Oh! The report is available?" Her family must have assumed I had access to it, or she had shared it, but that was not the case. Fortunately, autopsy reports are public records, and I had the necessary information required to request it. God bless government modernization, because it was emailed to me free of charge almost immediately after I filed the request.

The autopsy concluded that he had died from ingesting pentobarbital. There were other interesting items in the autopsy report, but mostly I was aware of how much Daniel would have hated it. The report described him as overweight and named his hair color as grey. This would have been cause for much pacing and affronted feelings if he were still alive.

***

My first big paperwork failure was trying to get refunded for the trip Daniel and I had planned to England and Scotland in March of that year. At first, I was able to transfer Daniel's plane ticket to another friend, and I planned to still take the trip with that friend, but later I decided I didn't want to. Having previously had luck at changing a major detail of the trip and having confirmed (I thought) that I could cancel, I made my decision. Immediately I couldn't get anything accomplished. Airbnb would not even refund half of my lodging. The airlines gave me the runaround. It seemed solvable, especially by contesting the charges with American Express before the trip was even scheduled to happen, since I hadn't yet used any of the things I had paid for. And yet, I ended up losing thousands of dollars in airfare and lodging I couldn't recover. The details seemed intensely important at the time, but ultimately there was no solving it. I hadn't purchased refundable tickets. I hadn't purchased trip insurance. This was just how it was going to be. No matter if I could prove someone else had already booked the Airbnb after I cancelled, still no refund for me.

***

There were also moments of grace and extreme generosity.

For the first week I thought of every one of Daniel's friends I could, and used my ingenuity to reach them, since most of the contacts were in Daniel's confiscated phone. I wanted to call the company that had laid him off to tell them he didn't make it through the particular adversity they had placed in his path, but I couldn't figure out where to start.

One sunny afternoon, I was pulling into the driveway at Daniel's to do more detective work and it hit me like a bolt of lightning that the only other person from Daniel's job I knew was someone Daniel had known before, and I had his number in my phone from a joint stargazing activity we did. I called the co-worker, a man named Ashley, to deliver the bad news. Ashley and Daniel had gone walking together the weekend prior, the same weekend I had gone for sunny walks with him at two different parks. (Daniel was desperately trying to soak up sun and hoping his feet would find a path that his mind could not—some way forward in his life.)

Ashley was shaken at the news. He asked what he could do, and I said I'd like someone from the company to contact me about working out a way for me to continue to access his soon-to-expire health benefits. The severance package at the layoff was a pittance: a few weeks of pay, health insurance through the end of the next month, and the ability to use the COBRA law to pay the full premium for up to 18 months. The premiums were going to be expensive, I knew, but my boys and I were all dependent on it for our health coverage.

Ashley called me back the next day. He said the CEO of the company was told what happened, and he was quite upset. Nothing like this had ever happened in the company. They wanted to be sure the kids and I did not have to worry about health insurance at this time, so they voluntarily covered our COBRA premiums for six months! There was still paperwork to be done because the "named insured" was no longer a valid human, legally, so new cards were issued in my name with a different number, which resulted in some problems later. But that was a tiny speck on the bright star of my huge gratitude to Tanium for stepping up in that way and to Ashley for advocating for me.

Later in the year, I would get a true demonstration of how Ashley could get things done. Daniel owned several shares of company stock, and I had asked about them. There were a few weeks of back-and-forth about whether I wanted to sell them back to the company, sell to a private buyer, or hold them. Then there was an issue with needing to transfer them into my name. Then there was a technical glitch with the tracking software. After a few months had gone by and my attorney was ready to close the estate, the Tanium shares were still not resolved. I sent a few strongly worded emails to little effect.

Finally, one afternoon I called Ashley and told him I was having trouble moving the stock sale along. First thing the next morning, the shares were ready to be moved into my name and cashed out. It was as if boulders had been rolled out of the way and suddenly it was a smooth and easy path.

***

Most of the path forward was considerably rocky. Some of the trouble was the suicide itself; suicide meant no life insurance to tide me over. Suicide meant the phone was confiscated for evidence. Some of the trouble was Daniel-specific, because he was so technologically and security-minded: He had a computerized thermostat, Ring doorbells, and an app-based home security system. I counted my blessings every day that nothing went wrong until I finally retrieved his phone from the police and could reset the passwords and access everything.

Some of the trouble was due to my lack of cognitive function. The temporary brain fog was real, and hard to manage. I needed every bit of my usual sharpness and critical thinking to navigate these extreme puzzles that even experts said they didn't know how to solve. But when I went to the well for ideas, the well was dry. I would try to buckle down, and there was just nothing there. It was highly unsettling, and inconvenient as hell.

Some of the trouble was plain old modern customer service, or lack thereof. Unfortunately, those were areas where I aimed my limitless wrath.

After talking to locksmiths who weren't optimistic about breaking into the gun safe, I contacted the safe company. They instructed me to fill out their "lock combination request form" for which I didn't have most of the answers. I gave up for a while. That was in early February.

A few weeks later, I circled back and sent a more agitated email explaining that I did not have the receipt for the safe, nor any way to prove I was a legitimate person to get into it. But I was named as the spouse on the death certificate, and I lived in the house, and the gun safe was in the house, and I'd like to get in.

What happened next was representative of so many of the tasks I tried to do at that time:

In April I wrote, "Hello, I was beginning to fill out your 'Combo Request' form. I noticed this: 'If you are not the original owner, and the safe has not been transferred into your name at

Liberty Safe, then a Bill of Sale will be required in addition to the information requested.'

I do not have the Bill of Sale. My spouse died and he was the only one with the combination. I am the executor of the estate. He has a file folder with the pamphlet for the safe, but no receipt or bill of sale. It may have been his father's gun safe. I'm not sure. Is there any way around this, or should I just try to find a locksmith who is willing to try destroying it to get in? I'd prefer not to destroy such a nice safe."

I attached Daniel's death certificate to the email. The same day, someone wrote back. "Fill out the form. Send in the executorship paperwork showing that you have the right to the safe combo and I already have the death certificate. We can get it for you that way," they wrote.

I returned the email with the executor paperwork attached, and the "combo request form," which of course had to be notarized. I have never had so many pieces of paper notarized as I did during this period of my life. Three days later, I received this:

"Alice, we received you [sic] combo request form. However, we cannot process it due to the form is filled out in the deceased man's name. Can you please resubmit the form in your name also. We need to have a copy of the death certificate." (Recall that the email from February had assured me they already had the death certificate.)

These were the kinds of circumstances that would have been frustrating normally, but now they absolutely made my blood boil. At the same time, most of the people I could talk to didn't want to hear about these clerical quagmires that were consuming my life. They wanted to talk about how much they missed this sweet, gentle man. For me, he was becoming a sweet, gentle man who could not possibly have made things more difficult for me if he tried.

Two hours later, I wrote back: "Hello, I have a question—Are you saying I should put *my* name as the 'owner'? That is not correct. I am not the owner. The owner is deceased. I am the executor of the estate. I cannot swear before a notary that the form is true and correct if I list myself as the owner. Also your previous email stated you already had the death certificate (See below) but I am attaching anyway."

A full week passed with no reply. I sent a nudge.

One day later, I received an email: "Since you are listed as the executor I went ahead and processed it. Please understand that since he passed away and you are the executor you are the legal owner of that safe. That is why we were requesting the form in your name. That safe is now in your name. Here is the information that you requested."

Attached was a PDF containing the combination that the safe was originally programmed with. Daniel never uses the default password or code for anything, so I figured there was a 30% chance of it working. I went into the closet and, for the first time in my life, took hold of the combination lock on the gun safe.

Turn the dial to the left four times, then stop at this number.
Turn the dial to the right three times, then stop at this number.
Turn the dial to the left twice, then stop at this number.
Turn the dial to the right until the dial stops at this number.
I turned the handle.
The door swung open.

It was a moment of great elation because I had been working for four and a half months to get the safe open. But there was nothing in there I needed by now. There were some file folders that contained long diatribes on why the network was set up the way it was, and how to configure the printer. There were rifles and pistols from his father's gun collection that he barely cleaned and never fired. There was a little bit of ammunition on the safe's floor, along with a box I hadn't seen before.

When I picked up the box, my heart dropped. It had writing indicating it was from Mexico and for veterinary use only. Inside was a nearly empty bottle of pentobarbital with just a few drops left at the bottom.

I don't know why the bottle and the box were in the gun safe. For whatever reason, he had locked up the empty bottle after drinking it or after pouring it into a cup. Maybe he thought if someone discovered the poison before it killed him, they might come up with an antidote and try to prevent his death.

I had researched this drug when the toxicology report came back, included in the final autopsy paperwork. It's what people use for assisted suicide in places where assisted suicide is not legal. It's the best, quickest, and most painless poison available. Terminally ill people around the world make pilgrimages to Mexico to buy it on the black market.

I don't know how Daniel obtained his. I do remember him talking about the "dark web" at one point a few years back. Maybe that's what he was doing on there. I am certain he had that bottle for a long time. I almost wonder if that's when things took the biggest turn for the worse. It's like when you know you're going to break up with someone, and you are already mentally moving on; there's no chance of things getting better. Once he bought that poison, he was already partially checked out, and it was always just a matter of whether this would be the day, or that would be the circumstance, that finally brought everything to a stop. Either way, I was holding it in my hand now. The weeks of wondering why there was no evidence of what he took to cause his death were over. Having the evidence didn't help.

I didn't feel as angry in that moment as I expected. I remember holding that box and the bottle inside it, and feeling profoundly sad. I was transported into Daniel's probable experience on his last night on earth, and I felt intensely close to him as I imagined him planning everything carefully, pacing frantically, his eyes red-rimmed and wild. That was the way he got when he was afraid. Like the morning he had to go to work on a top floor of a high-rise building downtown. Or the way he was when his computer crashed, and he thought his meticulously planned backup wasn't working right. I had seen him that way. I had held him, walked with him. Now I held the poison instead, as I imagined that last act of resolve: downing the whole thing in a couple of gulps, as I'm sure he did, and lying down to die.

I was so sad that he had to endure the horror of the most frightening of all liminal thresholds: leaving a life he knew as painful and terrible, and entering a death he couldn't know at all. I was gripped by the pain of not being there for him. I know of course he would have waited until I wasn't there. So not being there Saturday night didn't mean I was to blame. It would have happened whenever I was gone.

Remorse wasn't the main feeling. My primary impulse was wishing I could have held him and comforted him at the worst moment of his life, and for him not to be alone and afraid.

Eventually, I jerked back to the present and quietly put the box back in the safe.

Chapter 6

The Stories We Tell About Our Past

A funeral is supposed to be a way to say goodbye. You look inside yourself and find a place to put your grief, not somewhere hidden, not the top shelf or the back of a cupboard, but maybe by a window, where it can catch the light.

- Beth Lincoln, *A Dictionary of Scoundrels*

One of the most interesting things about going through someone's personal writings and letters is comparing the story they told about their life with the "primary source material" deceased people leave in their wake when they die.

When I felt drawn to "Daniel's house," (a year later, I don't call it that anymore), I would read the stacks of cards and look through the photos. On the weekends when my ex was with the kids at their house and I lived at Daniel's, I would grab boxes to go through.

Grief was a liminal, threshold experience for me, but also for the house. It wasn't Daniel's house anymore, but it wasn't yet mine. This was the truth psychologically, but also legally. The house belonged to the estate, and although the estate would eventually pass to me, for now I was a guest.

Once, his dear friend Paul came from out of town and we went through his office together. There were a few scrapbooks and boxes. Underneath a pile of papers inside a couple of envelopes, there was a letter he had written his mother and the letter she wrote back, which Daniel had torn into pieces but kept carefully in the original envelope.

There was a very long letter from a girlfriend he loved very much. He had shared with me an edited version of the things she said about him, the reasons she left, telling me they simply weren't true. Daniel said this girlfriend thought of him as mechanical and unfeeling, like a robot. I knew he wasn't robot-like, so I believed his indictment of his girlfriend.

But then I read her breakup letter.

It was compassionate. She saw him clearly. The things she noted about him were eloquently stated. Some of them pointed to habits he had since transcended, but others were things he and I had never fought about only because he started our relationship telling me they were non-negotiable. Armed with reams of evidence, apparently accumulated through arguments with his girlfriend, he created a space for himself where I had to agree and acquiesce, whether about home security or about our sex life. And because our relationship began that way, it was never a point of contention for me.

But the breakup letter was another interesting view on his world and his life. It fit into an alternate narrative that didn't exactly match the one he told me.

That made me reflect on how much we refine the origin stories of our lives over the years. Some people soften them. Some people sharpen them. Some people triumph over them. Some people become more and more the victim of the accidental crimes committed against them by their parents and siblings.

I kept exploring.

One day I decided the bedroom closet was worth a look. I really had no idea what was in there. Daniel had kept his clothes in the walk-in closet in the room he used as an office. I kept my clothes in the closet in my office. The closet in the room where we slept was…what was it for? It contained some spare bedding, and a bunch of boxes.

So, I began to open them.

There was a box full of old CDs.

There was a box full of martial arts belts.

There was a box full of sweaters. (I had never seen him wear a sweater. Not once.)

There was an old-school digital dictionary, of the same era as digital planners like Palm Pilots.

Then there was a box full of letters and photos and a big black binder. The black binder was filled with journal entries marked with "star dates," like the captain's log from Star Trek. He had always had more than a fondness for that series and its spinoffs. He craved a world like that, where intelligence and ethics always won the day.

I started reading from the beginning, getting to know a teenaged Daniel who still believed in a Christian God, and had enormously angsty and passionate crushes on girls. But I was most interested in the exchanges with his parents—the old letters tucked in the pages, or his accounts of talks or correspondence with his mom and dad. A separate shoebox of letters from his parents' estate supplemented the picture with the other side of the conversation.

What surprised me most was the fun and silliness he had with his mom and the appreciation for nature he shared with his dad. It was nothing he had shared with me. The version of his childhood he told to me was nightmarish and lonely. He shared a house in rural upstate New York with his mom, dad, and older sister. There weren't many neighbors nearby, and what social interaction there was, was dominated by his older sister who often made him feel left out in the way older siblings do. He resented her in many ways, not least because she seemed never to have any chores, while Daniel had many.

Their house was heated with a woodburning furnace, and he and his father spent hours splitting, stacking, and moving wood for the winter. They repaired things together. They went hunting together, but that, too, was a horrendous experience, according to Daniel. His father, who was profoundly hard of hearing, couldn't tell that he was crashing through the woods and scaring off all the deer for miles as they walked to their hunting spot. Once they reached the tree stand and settled in, Daniel was always freezing and they never got a kill, mostly because his father made too much noise. His mother, in his telling, was always either actively on drugs, recovering from an overdose, or away at a rehab center where they would sometimes visit her. She was non-functional, never made dinner, and he once found her unconscious on the floor of her bedroom, with fresh stitches from a recent medical intervention and an empty bottle of alcohol-based mouthwash nearby.

Other tales of abandonment were more mundane. He told a story of riding his bike to the local pond in the summer to swim and having a very hard time riding back home. He said he realized when he was older that it was because he was so hungry and calorie deprived. He said the fridge in his childhood home always had food, but no one packed him a lunch or taught him how to pack one. It was one of those strange complaints he had; he felt entitled to having someone teach him everything. He was always angry that his dad hadn't taught him about homeownership before he died. I didn't share his sentiment since I've figured out most things on my own by watching other people or by reading. But he felt betrayed and abandoned from not having been nurtured more intentionally. He was a sensitive soul, and it made sense that little Danny would have craved more sympathetic, supportive and kind parenting. It was not the kind of parenting he got.

He harbored a bitterness about not getting a different childhood, and shared it often, whenever he felt stuck or victimized by life. He always referred to his parents as "my mother" and "my father"—never as Mom or Dad. He had me convinced his parents were unloving and cold.

So, I was surprised to find a letter from Daniel to his mom where he peppered his missive about school with playful requests for her to buy him a car. And I was even more surprised to find a letter from Daniel to his dad where he described all the spring flowers and wildlife (rabbits, butterflies, etc.), that he could see while walking about his college campus in Binghamton, NY. I read the journal over the course of two weeks, sometimes taking breaks to try to track down the names I found and let them know what happened.

There was an account of a suicide attempt that landed him in the hospital. (Later I found the heartbreaking letters from the hospital's department of collections, demanding payment from a young kid with a crappy job, to pay them back for pumping his stomach. I can't imagine. There were records showing he ultimately paid them in full.) He came out of that incident stronger, started seeing a therapist, and started asking his parents more questions about his childhood. He became more accusatory then, having gotten the impression that something happened to him that he couldn't recall.

The letter he had torn into pieces from his mom was her response to his plea to tell him if he was abused or if something traumatic had happened to him. She said he was only abused verbally, and that she didn't want to delve into his past or his traumatic memories because it would unearth her own, and she couldn't bear to do that. She requested a "superficial relationship like the one I have with Kathy" (his sister) where they could share their daily lives but keep things light. This response was a betrayal for Daniel, who never hesitated to dive into the icky messy stuff of life. I had always admired his resolve to face what needed to be faced.

Perhaps he needed to be just as willing to dive into the joyous memories, and languish in the wonder of happy childhood moments, but he wasn't willing.

During the same timeframe, he wrote letters to friends (on a printer with the feed holes along the edges), and mailed them, keeping copies for himself. He told them he wasn't talking to his parents much anymore because they wouldn't engage with his hard questions. He was angry.

On one trip home from college for the holidays, he arrived on his front porch sporting an earring in his left ear, and his father wouldn't let him inside. He went home with a friend instead, and he and his father didn't speak for many months. He took up residence with his best friend's family on breaks, and they unofficially adopted him.

He planned a trip to Japan to study martial arts, according to the journal. (He never went.) He moved from upstate New York to Evansville, Indiana, with a girlfriend, which sent him on the trajectory that led him to Columbus, Ohio, and ultimately to me.

The journal entries and copies of letters ended around the time he was weighing the move to Evansville. On the very last page were instructions from some past suicide attempt, noting which of his friends should get his collection of CDs, his favorite stuffed gorilla, his books, and his motorcycle. At the end it said, "If anyone finds a black binder containing my personal logs, please destroy it. It's not meant to be read by anyone."

I was stunned for a second, and then I started laughing. That was a crazy thing to put on the LAST page of a journal you didn't want anyone to read. A few weeks later I made a huge fire in the fire ring and burned the pages.

***

The stories he told me about his girlfriends that had evolved over the years were one thing. The stories he told about his parents were more central to how he coped with life, and how he blamed more and more of his unhappiness on his parents, even as the time gap between their deaths and the present day widened. By the end, most of his career had occurred after they were both deceased, yet he often blamed his work stress on his father's influencing him into the field of computer science and on his dad's demanding nature. Yet, there were none of those sentiments in his journal in college when he was finalizing his major course of study and looking for his first jobs in his field.

We all grow up and look back to find causes for the things that influenced our personalities. But I had a front-row seat to what happens when one allows those circumstances to take more and more ground instead of less and less.

The stories he told about himself were the most damaging of all. When he was younger, he wrote about being uncertain about himself and his beliefs. But there was an authentic Daniel-ness that came through. I always thought his clear understanding of personal integrity came from all the self-help work he did, whether it was Dale Carnegie or Landmark Worldwide or other personal development courses. But it was there in his journal at age 20. It was central. It was only later that he underscored and affirmed his fragile parts until they gained the foreground. It was in his 40s that his anxiety gained dominance over his sense of adventure and desire for novelty.

I remember him hiring an expensive personal coach when he was in his late 40s, and the coach recognized that his rigidity had such a stranglehold on Daniel that one of his homework assignments was to buy very slightly adventurous food: for example, to select a different flavor of hummus. I gave the coach credit for catching on to who Daniel was. Our weekly journeys to Whole Foods (always on Sunday afternoon or evening), were eerily predictable. The only variables came from how much of something we already had in stock at home.

Looking back, it seemed he was more attached to a negative view of his life than anything else, including me. Early in our relationship, when feelings of love were running high, he would tell me that he was living and acting more from his "right brain" and able to be creative and loving, rather than existing mostly in his logical left brain. Having studied more about anxiety and depression, now I think it would be more accurate to say that he was hijacked by the fear and stress centered in his "reptile brain," the amygdala, preventing his higher mind from contributing more to his life and happiness.

As with most relationships, our early highs faded. But it wasn't just our relationship: Daniel was reluctant to celebrate promotions at work or victories elsewhere in life. He seemed to prefer focusing on fears and minimizing wins.

I always think of him when I hear the song "Rainbow" by Kacey Musgraves:

When it rains, it pours
But you didn't even notice it ain't rainin' anymore

> *It's hard to breathe when all you know is*
> *The struggle of stayin' above the risin' water line*
> *Well, the sky has finally opened*
> *The rain and wind stopped blowin'*
> *But you're stuck out in the same ol' storm again*
> *You hold tight to your umbrella*
> *Well, darlin', I'm just tryin' to tell ya*
> *That there's always been a rainbow hangin' over your head*
> *If you could see what I see, you'd be blinded by the colors*
> *Yellow, red, and orange, and green, and at least a million others*
> *So tie up the bow, take off your coat, and take a look around*
> *'Cause the sky has finally opened*
> *The rain and wind stopped blowin'*
> *But you're stuck out in the same ol' storm again*
> *You hold tight to your umbrella*
> *Well, darlin', I'm just tryin' to tell ya*
> *That there's always been a rainbow hangin' over your head*

When my kids were little, we read a Berenstain Bears book about bad habits, and the mother bear made a comparison to using a wheelbarrow along the same track, day after day. Eventually the track becomes a trench and it's very difficult to move the wheel off the usual path to the left or right, because the path is dug in. Daniel had dug himself in, quite effectively. Then he reaffirmed it over and over, locking down his habits, his home security, his routines.

I enabled it because I wanted to avoid conflict. I went along.

He praised me for honoring his sensitivities. If I questioned something, like why we needed to set the house alarm to go for a five-minute walk, he had a lengthy lecture at the ready, full of compelling evidence. After the second or third time, it wasn't worth it. I simply set the alarm.

And the trench became deeper.

He told himself stories about being anxious and rigid. And unloved by his parents. He became those stories. Then he persuaded all of us around him to believe and feed into them. We were all unwitting soldiers in the war he waged on himself. And he was the general.

It was a profound lesson for me, the power of the stories we tell ourselves.

Daniel's stories proved fatal.

Chapter 7

A Special Brand of Grief

> *Though Adam was a friend of mine, I did not know him long*
> *And when I stood myself beside him, I never thought I was as strong*
> *Still it seems he stopped his singing in the middle of his song*
> *Well I'm not the one to say I know, but I'm hoping he was wrong*
>
> - Jackson Browne, *Adam*

    I give a lot of credit to the suicide grief support group I joined. First because they sought me out just enough. They sent me a care package. They called. But they were not pushy. They knew that at the point when I was ready, I would join whichever modality was right for me: an online information workshop, a Zoom community gathering, or a 10-week, in-person support group.

    At least in my city, there is a whole entire support system just for suicide grief run by an organization called LOSS. I never knew there was any such thing. They are funded in part by the mental health board, which means they had a budget to send me some books and to pay for a meeting space for the support group. I never thought much about support groups. They seemed like a nice idea. I know people in Alcoholics Anonymous or other 12-Step Programs who value the groups very much. I had heard of other kinds of support groups. I thought, "Great! Good idea!" and then never thought about it again.

    What I didn't understand about support groups, even though it was the number one thing people said to me about them, was the importance of having a group of people going through a similar experience. I had heard that lots of times. What I understand now that I didn't before is that when something really bad happens, the amount of energy and patience I have available to explain it to people is minimal. It's hugely valuable to be able to skip over explaining things and magically jump to a deeper level of discussion. It means being able to examine and move through grief, without first giving someone a primer about the ground I'm standing on.

Once a week I had the privilege of being in a circle of other people who needed no background or explanation. We were all there for the same thing, and we all were the surviving family, friends, and spouses of people who left this world without giving us a chance to ask our final questions, or hover at their bedside, or say goodbye.

We were the people who found someone dead who didn't die because their body failed them. We were the survivors, widows, widowers, children, parents of people who died suddenly and unexpectedly, but with no reckless driver or ruthless murderer to blame. We were grieving the person we loved, and that person was also the person who killed the person we loved.

It was confusing.

Almost every death leaves some anger in its wake, often anger at being denied more time with our loved one. Suicide death comes with extra anger. Many of us are angry at the person who took their own life. I was also angry about what was left behind to handle, and how I was treated by law enforcement, the coroner, the bank, the credit card companies, the life insurance company, and the probate court.

Suicide death is also a surprise, by nature. In the United States at least, most people can't take their own lives with loved ones by their side. They must wait until they are alone and uninterrupted. Then we find them later. My surprise wasn't a graphic spectacle as some are, but I was still left fearful of more surprises.

Previously a highly social person, I found that my stomach was in knots if I went to a crowded place such as the theater or a luncheon. It seemed like anything could happen, and I didn't want any more surprises. If a car drove past in the rain and water splattered loudly on my windshield, it nearly sent me through the roof. To say I was jumpy would be an understatement, but that was what I told people. I minimized the fear I was feeling because it didn't make a lot of sense, and I was afraid people would crowd in and tell me to medicate or move my grief process to a clinical practitioner, and I didn't have the capacity to make those decisions. I lacked the mental bandwidth to consider the pros and cons of taking anti-anxiety meds or anti-depressants. I could not have chosen a psychiatrist or a new therapist.

I know my inability to handle medical paperwork was real because I tried to schedule a grief counselor for the kids and possibly for all of us together in a family counseling session. I called the insurance company as well as the Employee Assistance Program at Daniel's former employer, which was available to us because we were on his insurance plan. Each provided a list of counselors, many of whom were not nearby. My ability to sort the list and choose was frustratingly offline. This kind of task was usually easy for me. But it just wasn't working. I narrowed it down to the five closest ones and called all of them. The kids were 18 and 16 at the time and two of the counselors didn't take children under 18. Two more didn't do family counseling if the kids were 18 or older. Another was not taking any new clients.

I tried the other list and had similar results. Instead of feeling the normal resolve to conquer this persistent challenge, I felt angry and hopeless. I gave up on the lists.

I emailed the high school, which had been very supportive from the start via the school counselor. It seemed like they were already doing all they could, but my friends continuously asked (in a sort of ominous voice), "How are the kids doing?" So, I sent another note.

I knew I was distracted at home and probably not supporting them well, and I couldn't line up a counselor that was covered by insurance. I was at the end of my rope on this issue. Every time I went for a jog from Daniel's house, I would look around me on the bike path hoping today would be one of those rare times I crossed paths with the superintendent of schools, a fellow marathon runner. I imagined myself stopping him and telling him what had happened, and seeing if he had any ideas. For whatever reason, I thought that's how it should go.

One day I came to my senses and realized I could do that thing I hardly ever do, and I simply emailed the superintendent. My email was titled, "Making sure my kids are OK." Thank goodness I did, because it turned out there was an additional track of support at school through the school social worker, which I knew nothing about. Once I was in touch with the social worker, I learned that a local nonprofit would bring grief counselors TO THE SCHOOL and pull my kids out of class for grief counseling. In-school counseling was a huge win because I didn't have to keep track of anything, nor drive anyone anywhere. Later the school formed a grief support group at the high school—a resource that used to exist but was suspended during the COVID lockdown and hadn't been resumed. It made me feel good that other kids would receive support, too.

***

For myself, I joined the 10-week grief support group at LOSS. The first time I drove there, I noticed the organization's staff thoughtfully put a bunch of directional signs outside, so I was reassured I was at the right place, and they had a volunteer in the parking lot who told me which way to go. They knew what they were doing. We all looked like zombies and were likely to just get back in the car and go home if we encountered any obstacles.

We sat in a softly lit room with lots of snacks and water and a circle of chairs, with books and a pack of tissues at each seat. Over the weeks I got to know my groupmates. There were parents of children who died by suicide. There were adult children of parents who died by suicide. There were spouses. There were siblings. We had little else in common other than the most important thing in our lives right then. Someone who was probably politically conservative was sitting next to a woman whose deceased child identified as nonbinary and used the pronouns "they" and "them." There was no discussion about these things at all. There were religious people and non-religious people. It mattered only insofar as identifying whether religion was a resource a person could turn to. Unfortunately for some, their churches told them that their loved one had committed a mortal sin and were condemned to hell.

For me, the group was a place where I could say wildly impolite things and people would understand. I could admit that I was mad and sad, but also that my life was notably more positive and freer without the company of someone who was desperately anxious and depressed, someone who wanted my company as much as I could give it but didn't want to do anything or go anywhere.

Most of my daily interactions in the wider world were with people who wanted to reminisce about Daniel's great qualities: how he was a sensitive soul, and how much he helped others to understand the difficult technical topics he researched, so they wouldn't go through the same challenges. Most people wanted to talk about how great he was, and they were grieving too, so there wasn't an opening for me to talk about how angry I was that someone that smart and well-resourced couldn't shake himself out of his irrational thoughts. There weren't a lot of people I felt I could talk to about my emotions when I read the warm letters to and from his parents that painted a completely different picture than the awful childhood he blamed for his unhappiness.

The support group was a place where I could say anything. There were people like me for whom the grief was fresh and raw. There were others who had come back a few years out from the death because they were still struggling with unresolved anger, sadness, and questions. There were people who didn't get a suicide note and were left wondering. There were people for whom the suicide was such a surprise, they thought maybe there was some sort of mistake. There were others of us whose loved ones had been circling the suicide conversation for years, or who had made multiple attempts before they were "successful."

I pondered the different types of loss, even among this specific group. Children who lost their parents were abandoned in a very final way. It was not as if their parents were taken tragically in an accident. They chose to go.

Spouses—we were left. We were left like a breakup where we didn't get to send a text or tentatively ask for a phone call a week later or contemplate getting back together. We apparently weren't good enough to make a life worth living.

Parents who lost their children to suicide had made an investment in a young person with all the years of toil and work and worry and joy that every parent invests in their progeny. Instead of getting to watch their child grow up and thrive and create their own life, they saw their child conclude, with a brain not yet developed enough to make a wise choice, that life was not going to get better, or it wasn't going to get better quickly enough, and that this was where they drew the line. Parents who had once decided what food went into their child's mouth and what clothes they wore were now rendered utterly powerless over the most important decision there is and left empty-handed and broken-hearted.

For siblings who lost someone so much like themselves, it left them wondering if they were innately more vulnerable to suicide. They seemed burdened with being the surviving child and living out the potential of their deceased sibling, while also being overlooked amid their parents' grief.

***

Another aspect of my inner turmoil came from a profound sense of disapproval by Daniel. It seemed to me that nothing could more clearly indicate his disdain for me and our life than leaving it permanently. For me, it created the pervasive thought that I had done things wrong—irreversibly wrong. Even though Daniel was gone, I continued to carry his judgment with me. Anytime I did something at the house against his "rules," I was haunted by the criticism of his voice in my head.

I wasn't keeping the bird feeders full.

I sometimes ran upstairs to grab a forgotten item without first removing my shoes.

I baked a dessert in the kitchen and got flour everywhere.

I had not managed to source entirely organic food for the memorial event.

And so on, endlessly. It made it more difficult to grieve the loss of a caring, beautiful man, because the most frequent experience of him in my mind was a voice of reproach.

One day, I received a call from Della, a woman who led a transformational communications course I had completed years before. She was calling to offer her condolences and support. I can't remember what question she asked that provoked me to confess this experience: when I thought of Daniel, or tried to talk to him in my head, it was always in the context of me falling short of his expectations.

Della reflected back to me that I was constantly hearing from the version of Daniel that he had been toward the end of his life.

Yes, that was it exactly. I hadn't been in touch with the Daniel from the old days: the tender smile, the bright blue eyes, the intense interest in living things and in music and in me.

She asked me to think about what his ideals were when he was at his best.

I listed off some of the things he valued: compassion, a love of nature, an appreciation of beauty, and a commitment to people thriving and being their best.

Della encouraged me to imagine that version of Daniel in my head, and to think about what he might want for me. That was the first time I thought that he would want me to be free and happy. I thought that if there is something after this life, and if Daniel's consciousness endured somehow, he would actually be happy to see me casting caution to the wind and walking on the carpet in shoes or leaving the garage door open to go on a walk. He would understand that the rigid structures and rules he had in life were a compensation for fears that no longer troubled him. Relief rushed through me.

At Della's suggestion, I wrote the list of his ideals on a whiteboard in the kitchen, where they remain today. I still sometimes encounter thoughts of his disapproval, but each time I do, I remember what he valued and know that he would want me to have joy and love and freedom in my life.

***

Suicide is strangely contagious, and up until Daniel's death, I never understood why. The risk of suicide increases for those who have had a loved one take their life. After I experienced it, I finally understood more deeply. As the closest person to him, I not only knew intimately what he was thinking and feeling, I could easily step into his shoes and imagine those thoughts and feelings as if they were mine. There they were inside me. Visceral.

Further, I could easily see how the act itself was done, in practical terms. Many of the barriers are in figuring out the method, but that work had been done for me. Last, I saw the peace he was after. Sure, I was still here, left planning a memorial and shouldering the bills at his house, but Daniel was no longer suffering. He was not concerned with his salary, nor the condition of the roof, nor the state of Earth's climate, nor the trajectory of humankind. He simply didn't perceive any of that anymore, and in the throes of grief and handling an estate and running a business with half my brain shut down, dying sometimes seemed like a very peaceful and simple option that would solve all of my problems at once. I had an up close and personal look at how thoroughly death solves the problems of the dead person and transfers them to the living.

I wouldn't say I had any serious suicidal ideations, but I did have intrusive thoughts about it. Sometimes living just seemed too hard.

After those first few weeks when support was very high and expectations were very low, as the routines of life began to return to normal, I fell into a "functional depression." I found myself stuck in strange mental ruts that lasted days or weeks. My sales at work were poor, and when I asked for advice about how to have better sales calls, I often ended up in tears. My mind was telling me that I couldn't get better, or that I didn't want to get better, or that I deserved to be failing and miserable. I understood that it was a mental cycle, but I simply could not get out.

Worse, I had always had good mental health, so I was frightened and didn't know what to do for myself. Just like the temporary lack of cognitive function spooked me because I had always been able to rely on my intellectual sharpness, I was unsettled by having an emotional experience that didn't resolve with a good night's sleep or by going for a run on a sunny day. Nothing helped. I didn't *want* anything to help. I was in pain, and I welcomed the pain, and resisted anything that would turn it around.

Luckily, I was functional, and my kids had their basic needs met and I kept paying the mortgages and funding my employees' paychecks. But it wasn't much of a life at those times. The most empowering label I could put on myself, with the help of a coach, was "sad but strong." Whatever lesson the universe wanted me to get from Daniel's death, I guess I wasn't getting it, because the challenges kept piling on.

In March of that year, I finally made time to go to the dentist to ask about my aching tooth and gum. After a lifetime of uneventful dental cleanings, this was the year I endured seven months of specialist visits, including gum surgery and a root canal.

My younger son, whom I've always trusted to be competent with dangerous things like fire, tools, and sharp knives, wrecked two cars before his 17th birthday, resulting in trips to court, insurance claims, community service hours, body work on the car and fortunately, no injuries.

My older son was so anxious about choosing the wrong college he avoided the topic altogether, frustratingly, for months. It was on my shoulders to gently goad him into incremental steps to a decision.

In July, the beautiful car I had owned for three years was totaled. It had mostly been a symbol—a symbol that the goal I had for years to own a Tesla could come true. It was a symbol that I was successful and not to be trifled with. It was a symbol that I belonged with people who were doing big things. And then, in the blink of an eye, someone plowed into the back of me in a freeway traffic jam and I was relegated to driving a 20-year-old Toyota. Of course, the car I drive shouldn't define me, but the fact was that it had. The things that had been propping up my self-confidence were being taken away. I didn't replace the Tesla. Instead, I used the insurance payout for bills, pouring the unanticipated income onto the brushfire of expenses.

I felt like I was rolling downhill with nothing to stop me, and the hits kept coming. Sometimes I would yearn for someone to take my hand and say, "Okay. You passed. You've weathered all these things. Here's $20,000 and two days off work and a quiet bath." But no. No one ever did that.

I was continuing to throw everything at my emotional health, committed as hell to moving through the grief process. I had personal coaching from two coaches at once, the support group, books, exercise, meditation, yoga, massage, and more. I registered for a transformational training course, even though I'd done a lot of that work in the past. I needed a fresh dose, and someone I trust recommended a new version that was more experiential.

Eventually something shifted. I woke up one morning with a little twinkle of hope that something might get better, and I might actually have more business revenues this month than the month before, and maybe nothing else big would go wrong.

I was nearing the end of the lonely path of liminality, where my journey met back up with the rest of the world.

+++

PHASE: Integration

> ACTION ITEM: Check in with your loved ones on uncomfortable topics including finances. Even if you don't want to lend money, you can provide valuable counsel. The person experiencing loss may be hesitant to broach the topic but will be relieved if you do.

> ACTION ITEM: Don't be shy to research and recommend healing modalities such as counseling, support groups, somatic therapy and more. Provide the times, dates and costs and support where you can, but don't push. Make sure the information is ready when your loved one is ready for it.

A New Grief Model

A common complaint among those navigating grief is that their loved ones try to pigeonhole them into the Five Stages model of grief discussed earlier. In fact, Kübler-Ross derived the five stages of grief from interviews with people who had been diagnosed with terminal illness. These were the emotions people commonly reported wrestling with about their *own* impending deaths. Later, these same five stages were projected onto all of humanity, even though the experience of dying and the experience of losing someone are profoundly different.

When I learned this fact while reading, "The Grieving Brain," by Dr. Mary-Frances O'Connor, it made a lot of sense. Any human facing his or her own death would likely experience denial or resistance, since our primary instinct is to live. In fact, O'Connor (and others, including philosopher Jeff Foster), postulates that our thinking brains cannot truly conceive of our own death, since consciousness is derived from a state of being alive.

For me, and for many people who have the traumatic experience of coming upon the body of their loved one unexpectedly, we experience shock, but not denial. There was no room for denial in my experience. Daniel was absolutely, definitely lifeless in front of me. I could see and touch the lifelessness, and I did.

Researchers have recently discovered that what might end up categorized as denial or confusion is actually our brain's learning process. We have habituated ourselves to our loved one being alive. Many of our habits and daily interactions have involved this person. Even if our cognitive brain could process the concept of death, we haven't practiced what our day would be like without our loved one.

Quite the opposite.

We dance around each other in the kitchen to reach the garbage can or the tea pot. We check out of the corner of our eye to see whether their car is home. We can tell from a tiny corner of the bed visible through the doorway whether they slept well last night.

When someone dies unexpectedly, there is a learning process for the brain to integrate this new information. Daily habits all change. Sounds in the house change. This situation is less about denial than it is neural pathways, reinforced over years and sometimes decades, suddenly missing their usual inputs.

When I see a man wearing Levi's and a black T-shirt walking across the end of the reservoir near my house, I think it's Daniel because my brain is used to drawing that conclusion—not because I'm in denial that Daniel is gone forever. This confusion about the denial stage is just one example of why many people are searching for a new model to make sense of their grief, and why it doesn't help for friends and family to try to force a survivor into the Five Stages they once memorized.

Most researchers and counselors have now adopted the Dual Process Model of Coping with Bereavement, which is not a pathway of five stages to move through, but two types of grief processes people oscillate between: Loss-oriented grief activities and Restoration-oriented grief activities.

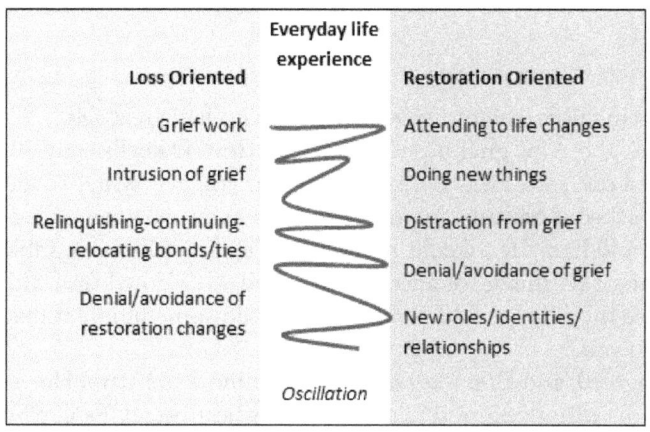

Stroebe, M., & Schut, H. (2010) *OMEGA-Journal of Death and Dying*

However, the Kübler-Ross model remains popular among the general public perhaps because so many of us were quizzed on it in high school. O'Connor's book takes a hard look at why we are still so attached to the five stages model. Her answer is the five stages mirror the "hero's story" where a person encounters a challenge, moves through a journey, and emerges transformed or restored. Although

Kübler-Ross herself insisted the stages need not be sequential, many lay people think they are to be encountered in order. Often, we do emerge from grief wiser and transformed, but it requires allowing ourselves to face toward grief, face away from it, face it again, and repeat for as long as it takes. In the beginning, there's not much time to face away, because the experience consumes everything. In the middle, we can take breaks, absorb ourselves in other pursuits or indulge in activities we had been putting off. Later, we don't need to distract ourselves anymore, and when grief arrives at the door, we can welcome it in, experience it, and move on.

For the bereaved and those who care for them, it's helpful to understand this "oscillating" Dual Process Model, particularly after the shock has passed, when the grieving person is working through the integration phase. Many clinicians, trauma-informed coaches and counselors are confident in words and actions that are supportive during each of the phases. They are comfortable talking to people who have experienced loss.

What if all of us could be?

***

I remember one of Daniel's friends who had great self-awareness about his grief process. A friend from Daniel's early 20s, Eric, lived one state away but kept in regular contact. When I called him and asked if he had a minute to talk, he knew what happened before I told him. He asked if he could travel to our home in Ohio to help clean or fix things, or anything I needed. "It's how I deal with things like this," he said. "I need to actively do something…if that's okay with you."

I agreed, and Eric was on the road within a few days. He brought his wife along, and I called Daniel's best friend, Paul, who also came to the house with his wife. I didn't know what chores I could give them, but I welcomed the company.

Once they all arrived, they quickly found things to do that didn't require much direction from me. I remember them cleaning out the fridge, handling the work of tossing expired food and wiping down the shelves. There was an occasional question, but mostly they worked away independently while I stood a few yards away, leafing through a pile of Christmas cards I found on a kitchen shelf.

Eric also volunteered to help me track down people I didn't

know and deliver the news to anyone whose name I didn't recognize, including someone who had mailed Daniel a Christmas card every year for at least a decade. (It turned out to be his ex-girlfriend's grandmother.)

Eric's story was a true win-win. His grief process was helped by being in service to me, and he knew how to do it in a way that was helpful without being an additional burden. I fondly remember taking a lunch break and sitting around the dining table telling Daniel stories and laughing and crying. Most people experiencing grief could use more people like Eric and Paul: unafraid, available, and present for anything from photo albums to spoiled milk.

It's "Simple": Don't Be Scared

When I had moved through the worst of my grief, I started noticing how easy it was for me to support others. What had shifted? Why was I suddenly eager to call a friend in need, instead of putting it off? Why was I no longer avoiding talking to people about loss, health setbacks, divorce, or estrangement?

At the heart of it was simple courage. I had just been through something horrific, so my standards for "comfortable conversation topics" had been completely reset. A normal day for me involved either a funeral home, police station, or attorney, and almost every day I needed to reveal and recount Daniel's death to a bureaucrat or customer service agent. The unintended consequence of this was that my resistance to difficult conversations about unpleasant topics decreased substantially. In fact, I became accustomed to such conversations. I took pride in putting the other person at ease. This shift in me made it very easy to pick up the phone anytime I heard a friend was going through a difficult time.

At the same time, I carried with me the special energy of someone who has faced shock and who has dwelt in the rare situation that cannot be repaired or ameliorated. It is a great sea of calm and acceptance, and people sense it. I noticed in the year after Daniel died, people would book a work meeting with me and end up baring their soul, confessing infidelity, confiding in me about a vast childhood hurt, exposing their helplessness and shame.

Their vulnerability was not the result of anything I had said. In some cases, the person didn't even know anything had happened in my life. I had involuntarily become a vessel for compassion and non-judgment.

I always leaned in.

I never recoiled.

Chapter 8

Thoughts on "Prevention Media"

"... once the storm is over you won't remember how you made it through, how you managed to survive. You won't even be sure, in fact, whether the storm is really over. But one thing is certain. When you come out of the storm, you won't be the same person who walked in. That's what this storm's all about."

- Haruki Murakami, *Kafka on the Shore*

The thoughts I'm about to share relate to suicide prevention, but they can relate also to overdose prevention or any other kind of traumatic death that technically could have been prevented but wasn't.

For friends of those who are grieving, it's important to be sensitive around these designated prevention months that appear in media and social calendars, but sometimes not for the obvious reasons.

The reason suicide prevention month was hard for me to manage was not because it reminded me of Daniel's suicide. I already thought of that every day.

It was hard at a deeper level because the entire premise of the month is that suicide can be prevented, either in very simple ways, like telling someone we care about them, or noticing when someone is not doing well, or sometimes in dramatic ways, like approaching someone at the edge of a bridge or a building.

These savior moments DO happen, and people should not hesitate to tell someone that they are loved and that they matter. I have a friend who was deeply depressed and just about to take a lethal dose of medications when his father, to whom he hadn't spoken in a year, knocked on his front door and interrupted him. His dad had no idea that his son was struggling, and they talked, and my friend got help, and now he's doing well.

It's not that I think there's something wrong with suicide prevention. The reality is that there are only a fraction of suicides that are preventable in that way. Take homelessness as an analogy. There are people who survive paycheck-to-paycheck, and they get hit by an unexpected expense and end up on the street. Given a chance, they can climb back up and maintain a home again. And then there are people who live on the street or camp on the land because they don't want to play the games of capitalism, or their mental illness prevents them from living independently in an apartment or from trusting people enough to participate in society. These folks are very unlikely to get back into housing and be able to stay there. Many don't want to.

There is a similar landscape with suicide. There are people who want to feel better and are searching for a solution to their anguish. And then there are people whose neural pathways have become so attuned to despair and negativity that it's the only road that exists for them.

I suspect Daniel bought that bottle of veterinary medicine a few years before he died. Once he knew it was there at the ready, he was just waiting for something to come along that was bad enough to justify tipping back that bottle. He had talked about suicide and tried suicide almost from the time he could contemplate his own mortality. His college letters said the reason that he hadn't gone through with it earlier is that he had been a serious Christian and believed in a literal hell that he feared would be worse than his unhappy existence on earth. Once he stopped believing in the revealed religions, he had less hesitation holding him back. After that, he stopped short either because he couldn't bring himself to do it (like the one night when he tried cutting an artery), or because he didn't want to leave a big mess or make life very hard for those he was leaving behind. He gradually solved these challenges over time, first by planning to shoot himself in the head with a motorcycle helmet on, in the bathtub (to reduce the mess), and then later by researching and obtaining pentobarbital.

Regarding those he left behind, he had my acknowledgement that (hypothetically), his death would be upsetting and then I would get on with my life. I mean, I have children. What else would I do?

Of course, I had no idea how upsetting it would really be, nor the emotional, physical, mental, and financial ramifications that would impact my life. But yes, I had agreed with him that I would ultimately be okay if something happened to him. I always am.

The reaction I had when Suicide Prevention Month rolled around was that every social media post seemed to imply I had not done enough. It was the same feeling I had in the early days after his death, when I would call friends to deliver the bad news and they would say something like, "Oh my god. He texted me last week and I didn't text back." As if a text would have wiped away years of declining mental health.

I couldn't solve it even with constant compassion, frequent encouragement, countless walks, innumerable hugs and indulgences of his wants and needs, helping him with a job search after the layoff and laying out a lower-income life plan. Because of the extraordinary effort I put in, it was upsetting to have people imply that a single text would have snatched Daniel from the gaping maw of despair. And it was unnerving to have people invoke Daniel's name in the same sentence as suicide prevention, as if we could have deterred him.

I know they didn't mean it that way. It's natural to feel guilty, to center on your own experience, and to think if you had done a little more it would have made a difference. But in some cases, it just wouldn't make a difference. As his suicide note said, "No one could have done anything to help." That was the sad truth. I know, because I was closest to him, and I had already tried everything I could. The most comforting thing a friend said to me the day I found Daniel was, "This isn't your fault. You know that, right? His brain was broken. His brain was broken and there's nothing you could have done to fix it."

This isn't to say that suicide can't be prevented. But it can be prevented in the same way that addiction can be prevented: by wiring one's brain to recognize beauty and love and be content with what we already have.

Jackson Browne's song "Farther On" alludes to this habit of humans to always be striving for some better tomorrow, while missing the beauty and connection and love we walk past every day.

Now the distance leads me farther on
Though the reasons I once had are gone
I keep thinking I'll find what I'm looking for
In the sand beneath the dawn

But the angels are older
They can see that the sun's setting fast
They look over my shoulder
At the vision of paradise contained in the light of the past

And they lay down behind me
To sleep beside the road till the morning has come
Where they know they will find me
With my maps and my faith in the distance
Moving farther on

It's easier for some people than others to be grateful, to nurture contentment, and to delight in babies and spring blossoms. But it can be learned. It can be improved. With Daniel, I saw him gradually lose sight of beauty and love.

He would still "pat the mums" in the fall when we walked past pots of chrysanthemums, and he would still scoop up wooly bear caterpillars and let them crawl on his hands. But winter had set in, and there was nothing soft on the horizon.

Among his notes, I found a paper that described the timing of the first signs of spring, so he would remember that even though it seemed interminably gloomy and dead, during a certain week in March we would begin to hear spring peepers at night. He used to frantically motion me into the car and drive to the country in the early spring, parking near a pond and rolling the windows down to listen to the frogs—the first sign that the Midwest would recover once again and claw its way out of winter.

But as he grappled with the layoff and spiraled into a panic, it was only January. The sound of frogs and the blossoming of flowers were still months away.

After a few blows from life knocked the wind out of him that last year, even the most brilliant blasts of compassion couldn't get through. I remember one night about six weeks before he died, I was at my kids' house, sitting at the kitchen island. I had come home from a school play that my younger son, Michael, was involved in. My older son, Noah, came downstairs and asked how the play was. I said it was good.

Noah has a friend we'll call John who has severe cerebral palsy and uses a walker. John had a part in the play.

"Did you see John in the play?" Noah asked excitedly.

"Yes," I said.

"Was he good?" Noah asked.

"Yes, he was really good," I said.

Thoughts on "Prevention Media"

"John told me Michael puts his costume shoes on for him every night," Noah said, off-handedly.

I caught my breath.

Tears of joy sprung to my eyes as I imagined my athletic, popular son kneeling to push shoes onto the gnarled and malformed feet of Noah's friend John every night, simply because it was something that needed to be done and he could do it. Michael didn't mention it to anyone. He just did it because he's a good person.

I felt intense gratitude, and I thought to myself that I was complete as a mother, right there in that moment. If I never did anything else, and Michael never went to college or did anything "great" with his life, it was enough for me that David and I had raised a teen boy who simply knelt and handled John's shoes.

I was eager to share the story with Daniel, because I knew he was having a hard time seeing the good in the world. In the past, he would grab onto nuggets like these and hold them fast, like a tiny glow in the vast darkness. His face would light up and he would get teary eyed.

I didn't text it to him. I waited until I got to his house, and I looked him in the eye and told him the story.

"Hmm," he said, and then changed the subject.

The next day, I circled back, because I really wanted him to see what I saw.

I made sure he was paying attention, and I said, "Hey Love, when I told you that story last night about Noah's friend John…do you get it? I mean, can you imagine being a teenager and having a kid whose hands and feet are curled in on themselves, which can be kind of scary. Can you imagine as a young person, volunteering to get up close and personal to help that kid on with his shoes? I mean, I just think that says a lot about Michael and Noah for being friends with him and supporting him like that. It made me feel like, if I never do anything more as a parent, I've succeeded in raising kids who are good people," I said.

"Yeah, I guess so," he said.

That was it. No emotional reaction. No resonance of my joy and love and pride. Just nothing. He was already planning his move by then. Around the same time, he asked if I had gotten trip insurance when I booked our Scotland vacation. I hadn't.

It's easier to see the warning signs, looking back.

A couple of weeks later, we were driving to get breakfast

together and I was singing along to Dua Lipa's "We're Good." In hindsight, I should have changed the song. I could tell he was listening to the words and wondering if I meant them towards him.

> *I'm on an island*
> *Even when you're close*
> *Can't take the silence*
> *I'd rather be alone*
> *I think it's pretty plain and simple*
> *We gave it all we could*
> *It's time I wave goodbye from the window*
> *Let's end this like we should and say we're good.*

When the song ended, he suddenly brought up a trip we took to Montana six or seven years before, and the surprise gift I gave him back then. Early in our relationship, on a brunch date, he asked me about a goal or a place I wanted to visit. I don't even remember what goal I named, but he asked me to write it down. I asked him the same question, and he wrote "Bozeman" on a slip of paper. When we arrived home, he put it up on the fridge. We each agreed to take a step in the direction of our goal, and he scribbled, "Request time off from work" below the word Bozeman.

A year later, we researched the heck out of Montana, I received a robust primer from Daniel on all his travel anxieties, we agreed on an Airbnb in the middle of nowhere near the Flathead River, and, with the help of Xanax, we got Daniel onto an airplane.

Once in Montana, he relaxed like I had never seen him relax. He loved the sound of nothing. We found an old horse blanket and laid it out on the grass in the yard. I watched him relish lying in the grass listening to the wind and nothing else. No man-made sounds. No man-made smells. The rigid armor fell away, and so did his fussy behaviors. When we picked up the blanket to go inside, I started picking all the grass off it because I knew we would not be able to move on until it was completely clean. I was astonished when Daniel gave it quick shake, said, "Good enough!" and went inside.

In Montana, he was in touch with nature. He was expansive. He was funny. He was adaptable.

One night, we were making stew in the kitchen and decided red wine would make a good addition. We searched the map and found a gas station that sold cheap wine and beer 19 miles away. But

Thoughts on "Prevention Media"

it was scheduled to close in 20 minutes. We jumped in the rental car and he sped along the country roads smiling and laughing, screeching into the gas station before it closed to buy a four-pack of Sutter Home merlot single-serving bottles with twist-off caps. They were horrible and we laughed the whole time.

The next day I told him I had a surprise for him, but we had to drive to Bozeman for it. He insisted on knowing where we were going to set the GPS. I asked him if he remembered the part in *Zen and the Art of Motorcycle Maintenance* where Robert Persig and his son and their friends make a stop on their motorcycle journey to visit friends in Bozeman.

"Of course. The DeWeeses," said Daniel. He knew the book inside and out and referred to it as "ZaMM" for short.

"Well, we're going to the DeWeeses," I said.

"What do you mean?" he asked, open-mouthed.

"I mean, I called the DeWeeses when I was planning the trip, and they invited us over."

Daniel's eyes got huge. He couldn't believe it.

"How?"

I just smiled my knowing smile that I have when I pull off something amazing. We started driving east.

We arrived at the DeWeeses, and there they were, old but happy, pursuing their passions, and in no hurry about doing so.

We visited with them, like people did in the old days, and they showed us around. The best part was the "Be Deck." At first I thought they said, "The B Deck," as if there was an A Deck and a B Deck.

But no.

It was the "Be Deck" which was only to be used for "being" and not doing.

No doing was allowed.

Only being.

It was a magical place.

There were a couple of horses and a yurt, and I don't remember what else, but it was a better visit than I ever could have imagined. They were used to having ZaMM pilgrims now and then, although it was clear they didn't take all comers.

Now here we were years later in the Ohio winter, soaking in the rare sun as we drove to breakfast. The mood in the car had been tense, but a familiar kind of tense. It was a tension that said, "Neither of us can make the other happy. And we know the other is not happy."

Daniel looked over and said, "I really, really appreciated when you took me to the DeWeeses in Montana. That's probably the best gift anyone has ever given me."

I was surprised he was bringing it up out of the blue, but pleased to be acknowledged for something that had, in fact, required a lot of effort.

"You're welcome," I said, beaming.

In hindsight, I now realize he was saying goodbye, and that was the nicest thing he could think of to say to me.

***

His friends who have called and who have wrung their hands over their not-enoughness—at first, they made me angry. I was at the center of his life, so obviously it was my responsibility to solve it. To make Daniel happy. To fix him. And I had failed.

But after more time, more reflection, and some settling down, I realized he would have tipped back that bottle much sooner without me and the support of the rest of his friends. He had had one foot out the door for a very long time. Joy and beauty and trust became smaller and fainter and further away.

And then it was just dark all the time.

Still, he hung on.

But eventually, he could no longer see what he was hanging on for.

He put that bottle to his head and pulled the trigger
And finally drank away her memory
Life is short but this time it was bigger
Than the strength he had to get up off his knees.

- Brad Paisley, *Whiskey Lullaby*

***

I couldn't save Daniel, but I can save myself.

Maybe if I had taken him by the shoulders and shaken him, maybe if I had demanded that he look around at the beautiful hearts of my children, and the beautiful shapes of the tree trunks in the winter, and the beautiful dreams I had for the future, maybe it would have delayed things. But honestly, I don't think it would have turned things around. It takes an intentional shift in thinking, and a willingness on the part of the one thinking the thoughts.

Maybe it takes something to live for, as Viktor Frankl talks about in his book, *Man's Search for Meaning*. The ones who made it through the concentration camp had a wife to get back to, or a book to write, or children to find again.

Daniel had always resisted having those permanent responsibilities. He never wanted children of his own, though he was okay with liking mine. He loved dogs and fussed over them, but he let other people be the dog owners.

Having watched him, more than ever I understand the importance of having both feet in. I'm here for this life. I'm all in.

I'm here for my kids. I'm here for my friends. I'm here for my crazy dreams and trips I want to take and sunsets I want to see.

I have things to contribute to the world, and they mean something to me. It matters that they mean something to me—not objectively, but simply because I say so. The world from my view of things is the only world I'll ever know.

This consciousness that I experience, looking out of my eyes, it's the only one I'll have.

If I say my life matters, then it matters. What I think is really the only thing that matters to me, because my experience is the only one I have.

And when I die, my death won't matter to me because my consciousness and my meaning-making will expire with my last breath.

We each create meaning out of everything in life. Our brains are little meaning-making machines. That's what they do. They make up stories, they add significance, they engage in melodrama. If I'm going to create meaning, I'm going to create joy and grace.

I'm going to be fully alive, dammit. And I want everyone else

to be fully alive, too.
   That's what suicide prevention means to me.

Chapter 9

Ways to Support and Ways Not To, and It's Up to the Bereaved

The most beautiful people we have known are those who have known defeat, know suffering, known struggle, known loss, and have found their way out of the depths. These persons have an appreciation, a sensitivity, and an understanding of life that fills them with compassion, gentleness, and a deep loving concern. Beautiful people do not just happen.

- Dr. Elizabeth Kubler-Ross, Psychiatrist

Having gone through something disruptive and upsetting, I now have the privilege of being an expert at grief. I have complete confidence in how to handle myself around someone who is dealing with grief. It's a nice thing. And it came from experiencing things that worked incredibly well and things that didn't work at all.

I'm sharing these stories because everyone can learn to be a better friend. It's not something we necessarily have good instincts about, especially if we grew up in families where we all went to the funeral home and made sad faces and stood in line and prayed in front of the body and then went home and never spoke of it again.

Something that worked well was having people step in and take over at things they were good at.

David, my boys' dad, handled everything with the kids for a while. People would ask me how the kids were doing, and I would say, "I have no idea, you'll have to ask their dad." I couldn't see past my own nose and I just didn't have the capacity to figure out how they were doing and support them better. If I was keeping up with the mortgage, that was me doing my best at parenting right then.

Eventually I made my way through the hardest part and was engaged and actively supporting my eldest son in choosing a college and enrolling and applying for housing and all those important things. We

hosted a graduation party, and I bought balloons and set up tents. I didn't abdicate the role of mother. But for a few weeks there, I was not very aware of anything other than my own anger and my conversations with my support network.

My friend Aaron not only set up the Meal Train but included links to useful articles on supporting people in grief. This was great, because most people showed up at my door with dinner, on time, and well trained in being available but not overbearing. One of Aaron's helpful articles was about Ring Theory. Ring Theory, developed by psychologist Susan Silk, is best summed up with the phrase "comfort in, dump out." The premise is that the person closest to the grief, trauma or difficulty is at the center of concentric circles. The family and friends of that person are arranged farther out within circles around the center of grief.

The guidance from Silk is that supporters are to comfort those inward in the circle. When interacting with someone in a smaller circle closer to the grief, be a good listener. Bring neutrality and curiosity. Say things like, "This must be really hard for you." Or "Let me bring you dinner."

Remarks like, "Why me?" Or "I'm exhausted from this whole situation," should only be directed to people in a circle farther away from the center of the grief.

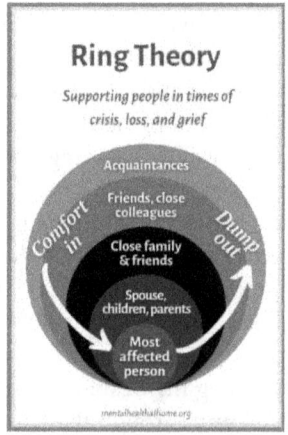

Susan Silk, *Los Angeles Times* (April 2013)

This simple diagram makes it easy to remember. It can be stressful to lean into a traumatic situation and comfort a friend. If you're nervous, it's natural to think of sharing your own "similar" story or to offer advice instead of just listening, reflecting back, and validating your friend's emotions.

Ways to Support and Ways Not To

Some people in my life did read the articles, like the one about Ring Theory, but still weren't up for talking about the actual difficult topic at hand. It wasn't bad, it was just what was real.

When people brought me Meal Train dinners, I usually invited them in, because I wanted someone for the kids and me to talk to. We needed company, first and foremost. People get weird when something tragic happens, and they assume they aren't part of the inner circle and therefore they should give the mourners their space. But that space gets lonely. At times, I felt like a social pariah. More accurately, I felt like an evil villainess from a Disney movie, with an imaginary black cloak trailing behind and beside me. When I walked into a room for business or a school function, it seemed like the lights dimmed a little and the music stopped. Everyone looked up, recognized me, and assumed a look of pity. Suffice it to say, having a thoughtful conversation or a warm reminiscence about Daniel in my kitchen was something I desired deeply.

Also, I believed it was important for the kids to have a chance to process and talk about Daniel, and it was easier to do that with other people around. But sometimes I could tell the guests who dropped off dinner were not up for it. Their eyes slid away from mine, and they looked like they were nervous that I might utter the word suicide. Some people were helpful and signed up for dinner, but we really weren't close at all and so seemed to lack the foundation for a difficult conversation. Others were too raw from their own recent loss and weren't healed enough to engage about mine. In each of those cases, I would let them off the hook with a quick smile, and I'd launch into talk about the college search, or pets, or some topic in their life.

On the other hand, there were some people I hardly knew, but I could clearly tell the foundation was firm for deep discussion. Those were often folks who had weather a loss or tragedy of their own and were deeply grounded. Their calm was contagious and helped me feel safe.

Either way, I didn't have to figure out what to make for dinner, which was wonderful. The Meal Train held many lessons, especially on the finer points of "emotional work" and decision fatigue.

For example, there were people who contacted me to ask a lot of questions, which I didn't really want to deal with. There were people who didn't pay attention to the instructions and brought food I preferred not to eat, or dropped it off on the wrong day because they didn't have room in their freezer (assuming that I would be able to absorb that duty), or forgot to set the delivery time for an online order and had it delivered in the afternoon so that I had to drive to the house mid-day to take it inside before the squirrels carried it off.

It sounds ungrateful to complain about these tiny missteps while people were providing our dinner. But the thing is, when I was deep in the throes of grief and I was using absolutely all my brain function just to keep the lights on, I truly did not want to manage someone else's dinner delivery issues.

One of the prime guidelines for dealing with grieving people is not to give them work. We have enough work. We are processing things emotionally, we are handling funeral arrangements, we are navigating interpersonal relationships with family members who may not get along with each other. We truly don't have the capacity to discuss at length whether we have a dairy allergy or just a preference not to eat cheese.

People do get nervous around grief, and they trip over themselves and create more awkwardness. It is almost always clumsiness that is the source of upsetting behavior, hardly ever malice. It's helpful to imagine the grieving person is on a fragile island made of tiny sticks woven together, and disturbances to the water or the stick platform will cause the person to get wet and cold. Please do talk to them and bring them dinner and support them in the ways they ask but try to do it without getting them any wetter. Minimize questions and decisions. Be calm and don't make waves.

A week or so after Daniel died, I had posted his obituary to a group chat of people I know from all around the Midwest, all of whom have taken advanced communications training. One of my friends from Detroit said she was planning to be in Columbus. She had seen my post and wondered if I'd like to have dinner with her that Friday. I said that would be great, because I didn't have much appetite and going out to a restaurant might help me eat better. I told her I had plans to go see live music later that evening, but I could meet her as long as we finished by 7pm. I figured this would work fine because she was planning to be near the convention center downtown, which would put me on my way to the music event in a rural area.

She asked me what restaurant I would suggest. I cringed a little because I didn't want to deal with logistics. I wanted people to care for me and set everything up and just hold me in their arms and deal with all of the hassles for me. But I took a deep breath and suggested an organic burger place near the convention center. I put it in my calendar for 6pm.

That night I was pulling into the parking garage at 5:50pm when she called. She was just getting off the freeway in the area and wanted me to send the address of the restaurant. I had already sent it, plus she could have Googled it, but I gave it to her again. Then I walked to the restaurant and got a table. Five minutes later she called and was a bit lost. Five minutes after that, she called and had parked, but got turned around finding the restaurant. In a moment of clarity, I gave her brilliant instructions. "Wendy," I said. "Can you see the convention center?"

"Yes," she said. "I'm right at the corner."

"Okay," I said. "If you keep the convention center on your left side and start walking, you are 100% certain to get to the restaurant. It will be on your right."

At this point I was very annoyed because she could have used GPS. Further, we were cutting into our dinner time and I was eager to be on time for the blues show. Also, I was agitated being in a busy place, and I was feeling conspicuous taking up a huge booth by myself. I felt very small and vulnerable, and the irrational jumpiness was rising in my body.

A couple minutes later, Wendy called again.

"I'm almost there, but since I'm running late, I wondered if you could do me a favor. I invited my friend Linda to join us, so could you look for her and let her know I'm almost there?"

I flipped out.

"Wendy, did you read the message I posted? Do you know what's going on with me?" I asked.

"Oh yes. Yes, I know," she said.

"Well, Wendy, I don't want to eat dinner with a stranger right now. I'm just not up for that. I don't want any surprises. I didn't know you were inviting anyone."

"Oh, okay, I understand," she said.

As it turned out, she and Linda arrived around the same time. They conferred, and then walked over to my booth. Wendy said, "I totally understand what you were saying on the phone. So, Linda and I are just going to get a table over there."

"What? You're going to leave me here alone?" I was

incredulous. She was seriously choosing her other friend and abandoning me after inviting me to dinner. Right in front of my face.

I gave up and invited them to my table. I was the one in a hurry, so I had already ordered fries and a vegan milkshake to go. I wasn't going to be there long, so my discomfort with Linda would be short-lived. Wendy and Linda took off their coats, slid into the booth, and then Wendy immediately began complaining about teaching school.

I looked up sharply and said, "Wendy, this is a No Complaining table."

She complied and changed the subject. She never asked about me, or Daniel, or how I was doing. Somehow, I ended up picking up their check, and leaving about 10 minutes later.

In hindsight, I suspect she had great intentions and wanted to reach out but became nervous about such a traumatic death. She may have been concerned about what to say to me about my loss, and nervous about doing it alone. Maybe that's why she invited a friend and why she got turned around walking from the parking garage.

Thankfully I was meeting a different friend to see the blues show, and that friend drove WAY out of town on a snowy night to meet me, didn't complain, listened thoughtfully, asked considerate questions, paid for my drinks, reassured me, and gave me a hug.

Now in this case, I was lucky because Wendy and I had been in a communications program together, so I knew I had an opening to talk it out and keep from holding a grudge.

After a week of telling this story to friends and realizing I was gossiping, I finally called Wendy and asked if I could give her some feedback and get some resolution on what happened. I recalled the sequence of events to her and asked if she could see how she was putting work on me (the grieving person), and being pretty insensitive generally. She agreed and apologized, and there were no hard feelings. She thanked me for being honest and giving her a chance to clear it up.

In addition to stories like this about what not to do, there are helpful tips floating around the social media, like the "Grief Groceries" post, which I will reprint here with attribution to the original author, Hugh Hollowell, Jr., originally published at his blog and newsletter, *HughHollowell.org*.

Ways to Support and Ways Not To

Grief is a funny thing. It's the time in our life when we most need help, and also the time when asking for help is so hard. Not because we are ashamed to ask for help, although that happens sometimes too. But mostly because our brain just sort of shuts down.

When my Dad died, I looked functional. But I wasn't OK. Not at all. And when the news got out, the ton of people flooding me with calls, texts, and DM's was overwhelming. I really couldn't function. I sat on the swing in our yard and just stared into space. People called and asked what they could do to help. I had no idea.

"Well, anything you need at all, let me know, OK?"

"OK".

They hung up. I stared into space some more.

I had no idea what to do. What I needed. I didn't even know what to ask for.

Then a friend sent a text. This friend had met Dad once but didn't really know him. But still, she knew I was hurting. I saw who it was and almost put the phone down without reading the text, but I saw the message and it stopped me:

Will you be home at 8:30 tonight?

What's weird is this friend lives 12 hours away from me.

Yes, I replied.

"K."

10 minutes later, she said, "Instacart will be there at 8:30. Open the door for them."

"What?"

"Grief Groceries!"

When Instacart showed up, they put two large bags of groceries on my porch. Frozen pizzas. Ice cream. Oreo cookies. Tinned soup. Stouffer's lasagna. A gallon of milk. Like that. Things I could heat up if I needed a meal, or pig out on if I needed fat and sugar. Sometimes, you just need to eat half a box of Oreos.

Notice she didn't ask if I needed any food. I would have said no. She just asked if I would be home.

Grief groceries.

Another friend, who lives out of town, asked Renee to name a restaurant near our house where we like to eat. There is a local chain near our house that is sort of a deli. When we eat supper there, we spend about $25. Renee told her the name of the place.

An hour later, there was a gift card in my inbox for $250. Yes, that is a lot of money, and I understand not everyone can do that. But the wonderful thing was that because it was enough for multiple meals, we didn't try to save it for "the right time". We ate there that night, and take out from there several times a week for the next month on nights when I just didn't have the spoons to cook.

Both of those gift-givers knew something I didn't know—that when you are grieving, you don't want to make decisions. No, that's not quite it: You can't make decisions. You hit decision fatigue really fast.

So, I guess what I'm saying is, don't ask grieving people to make big choices or decisions. "How can I help" is a big choice. But "Can I take the kids this afternoon so you can have some time to yourself" is a much smaller one. "Will you be home tonight?" is a small choice. "What restaurant do you like" is a small decision. Just showing up to cut their grass because you noticed it needed cutting is loads better than asking, "Do you want me to cut the grass?" Or, "I'm going to Target. What can I get you while I'm there?" is better than "Can I run any errands for you?"

It won't always be like this. If you stick around, eventually they will surface and ways to be helpful will make themselves known. But in the first few days, especially, it helps to remove as many decisions from their plate as you can!

+++

PHASE: Shock

ACTION ITEM: Determine something you'd like to do to help (provide dinner, complete a household chore, etc.), and then make all the arrangements you can on your own. When you've reached the point where you can't complete the action without input, ask the grieving person the most minimal questions possible, such as when a convenient time is to stop by.

ACTION ITEM: If you are able to communicate with other supporters of the person who has experienced a loss, share with them some best practices and tips such as Ring Theory, the Grief Groceries article, and information from this book.

Chapter 10

My Declaration

New Normal

i don't think we talk enough about how quiet the road gets. how long the waiting feels. how lonely healing can be. i don't think we talk enough about how undone we become in the valley of grief. or how enormously we must stretch just to fit ourselves into some kind of a new normal and dare to call it life again. and I don't think we talk enough about how we have no other thing left but to gather up our heavy limbs and carry on. because the earth keeps on spinning. the sun keeps on rising. and the days keep on bleeding, one into the next, regardless of the moment that made all the minutes inside of our heart stand still.

- Ullie-Kaye, Joy Trickles In

One of the best questions I received from people was, "Do you have something you're looking forward to?" It helped pull me out of the tailspin of what-if thoughts and focus on something ahead of me.

This helpful question should not follow immediately after, "I'm sorry for your loss." It's something to say a few days or weeks later, especially if the bereaved is showing listlessness, a heaviness, or a lack of will to live or move forward.

Fortunately, during my grief journey I had things to look forward to. With increasing frequency, I encountered an awareness that there would at least be breaks from my lonely liminal path and I would rejoin humanity.

First, I had a relay race coming up and my team of 10 runners needed me. Most of them lived an hour away, but all the women on the team came up one weekend morning to run with me and have breakfast together. It was touching and made me feel very supported.

Second, a couple weeks after Daniel died, I found out the nonprofit I co-founded had been awarded a half million dollars in operating funds by the city of Columbus. That buoyed my spirits.

I also had been gunning for a particularly prestigious award given annually by my women business owner's association. At some point in the blur of customer emails I didn't want to handle and estate tasks I didn't yet have the authority to handle, I received an email stating that I was being honored with the award. The two honorees were going to be filmed for a professionally produced video, and then would receive the awards at an in-person event and have a chance to make remarks.

At that time, I was still navigating how and when to discuss what had happened. It wasn't central to my work. It certainly wasn't aligned with the energy of the person calling to congratulate me, nor the energy of the video producer, who was brimming with fun ideas.

I scheduled the video shoot, agreed to wear a flashy cocktail dress, and acquiesced to the idea that I needed time for hair and makeup prior to arriving to the video session. Then I said carefully, "Listen, I think some of you may know this already, but I recently lost my life partner to suicide. I'm bringing it up because a lot of people know, and it would be weird not to mention it in my remarks, so that's when I'm going to talk about it. I think it will work well to show the video first and go ahead and be fun and joyous. And then I'll get around to this, but in a way that works in the space. It will be a little strained, but it would be even weirder to pretend it didn't happen."

I handled the planning with grace, and I truly enjoyed getting my hair and makeup professionally done, which I had never, ever done before, not even for my wedding in 1998. I looked amazing. I had great photos taken. I invited lots of people to the awards dinner.

Then I gave the speech of my life, because it was my chance to reconcile what happened to me with where I was going and leave no doubt in the minds of my supporters that I was not going to crawl into a cave. Here's what I said:

Listen, this is going to be more of a declaration than an acceptance, so I'm going to take a few minutes.

Thank you so much.

I'm thoroughly proud and honored to receive this award, especially knowing the caliber of previous awardees.

I understand and fully appreciate the importance and… dignity…of this honor, the NAWBO Visionary Award. And I am full of gratitude for the family and friends who supported me to get here.

My Declaration

It's been such a privilege to grow my company, SiteInSight, alongside the amazing members of this organization.

I'll admit, I didn't join right away.

I attend a lot of networking events, and sometimes I would attend an event where NAWBO Columbus was a partner. I was always impressed, and I understood that NAWBO Columbus represented women business owners defined by high-level performance and integrity. I knew NAWBO Columbus was the largest NAWBO chapter in the United States. I could recite their entire pitch. ... I wasn't quite sure I belonged here yet, honestly, but I was very attracted by the fact that NAWBO women are confident. They are…WE are successful. We operate from strength and self-assurance. We are amazing and we know we are leading strong companies. I remember telling my life partner, Daniel, about NAWBO, and right away he asked when I was going to join. I gave a wishy-washy answer with some lame objection about the annual membership fee. The next day, I found his trademark piece of an index card on my desk, bent into a little triangle, with Daniel's handwritten note: "Join NAWBO". I kept it there for a number of months until I finally filled out the application and wrote the check.

That was years ago now.

In between being nominated for the Visionary Award this winter, and being notified that I would be one of the honorees, as some of you know, I lost Daniel to suicide. Yeah, I anticipate the sound of that gasp now. It's become familiar. And I know that behind the faces wrinkled with sympathy there has been a real fear…a fear that I would fall apart, that I would quit work and let my company, SiteInSight, and my nonprofit efforts, especially Elevate Northland, founder. Interesting word. Founder. To founder, as a ship: To go down. To fail or break down. To descend into a body of water…to sink beneath the surface…to be ruined.

But also:

Founder: A person who establishes or creates something that is meant to last a long time. A person who got something started or caused it to be built. One who lays a foundation. And I would add, the person who takes initiative. The one who takes the risk. The one who says, "This WILL happen on my watch."

I choose that second definition of founder.

Death has many lessons to teach, and it's been a privilege to be its student.

I built a life with someone, and that man wrote in his suicide note that life wasn't good enough. (Yes, **that** life that we had together.) In fact, it was so painful and filled with suffering, oblivion was a better option. Nothing was a better option than this something that we had. For someone like me, often driven by a fear that I'm not good enough, there's no challenge more powerful to confront. If I can face such an ultimate declaration of my worst fear—not being good enough—I can certainly take a "no" from a sales prospect or a "try again next year" from a corporate foundation.

But a more profound lesson was to witness the power of the voice in my mind. You have that voice, too, and so did Daniel. Many seekers, philosophers, and spiritual leaders quietly repeat to us the wisdom that the voice in our mind … telling us that our joke fell flat,

that the group whispering over there in the corner is mocking us, that we'll never make it…

that voice, that bitter, cynical voice, is **not us,** they say. It's a defense mechanism to keep us safe and small in childhood, but there is no off switch…it doesn't shut up in adulthood.

These wise teachers, they tell us that our will, our commitment, our volition…it is stronger than the voice. But we listen to the voice. Sometimes, tragically, we listen only to the voice and lose sight of beauty and love and purpose. That's what happened to Daniel, the man who spurred me to join this group.

Grief has been an interesting thing.

And we **all** know grief. The death of a parent. The death of a beloved pet. The breakup of a relationship. Carefully laid plans obliterated by a mistake in some paperwork. Sudden emotional distance from our children or a previously dear friend.

Whatever the cause, the grief is a journey.

I've learned I can control my pace on this journey through this jungle of anger and sorrow and suddenly changed plans; I can walk faster or slower, but I can't control how long the path is. I've learned I can stop and sit down, but I'll still have just as much distance to cover when I get up again.

And I've learned that pity is like a very attractive swamp that pulls at my ankles. Oh, how nice it would be, knowing that no one would judge me for it,

to just

stop.

No one would say anything to me if I ran my online marketing company into the ground. Nothing but, "Poor Alice." No one would criticize me if I stopped building a business center and incubator for disadvantaged businesses in Northland. I can even imagine the news stories about a promising dream that fell apart when the founder…foundered. It was understandable. So tragic.

Don't get me wrong. This isn't a story about leaning in and working myself to the bone, and never stopping to cry.

I cry.

This is a story about a woman who saw what happened when someone listened too hard to that awful, destructive voice and stopped being able to Live

And Love

And leave a Legacy.

I don't want that for me.

I don't want that for YOU.

So, I'm in this period of...grace – yes, exactly a "grace period," where everyone says I can do anything I want: "It's OK, Alice. Take time for yourself." I could get a massage every day. I could buy a motorcycle again or move to Costa Rica. I could enter a monastery. I could immediately start dating someone new. (OK, I'm doing that one.) I could watch TV for days on end and eat pizza and ice cream for every meal. And most everyone would knowingly shake their heads and say how sad it was and tell me to keep doing whatever I want.

What is it that I want? As a person who is choosing to LIVE?

Think about that for yourself, too.

Because we are CHOOSING to wake up every day.

What I want now, what I **really** want after all of this,

Is to keep building my marketing company. To keep hiring and employing people who may not be neurotypical, but who are brilliant, creative, and integral to the team.

What I really want is to send my two boys, a junior and a senior at Westerville North, off to college with a sense of wonder and excitement, and the quiet knowledge that I have their backs.

What I really want is to turn run-down motels on Route 161 into beautiful buildings with affordable apartments and condos, attractive retail shops on the ground floor, and gardens and solar panels on the roofs.

What I really want is to take the $4 million dollar campaign for Elevate Northland from the halfway mark, which I've reached with the support of Mark Swepston, Cameron Mitchell, the City of Columbus, the Columbus Foundation and others, to the 100% mark. To cut the ribbon on a state-of-the-art community gathering space, rentable commercial kitchens, food truck parking, co-working and co warehousing in a community that is hungry for neighborhood resources, identity, and pride.

What I really want is to leave a legacy so big that the mean, critical voice in my mind is left, finally, speechless.

My Declaration

> So, since everyone keeps telling me I can do whatever I want right now, **that's**
>
> what I'm
>
> going
>
> to
>
> do.

+++

PHASE: Recovery

> ACTION ITEM: Ask the grieving person if they have something to look forward to. Support them in shifting their focus to the present and the future. Celebrate the wins with them so they know it's okay to experience joy.

Chapter 11

Finally, My Grief Exceeds My Anger

Let This Darkness Be a Bell Tower

Quiet friend who has come so far,
feel how your breathing makes more space around you.
Let this darkness be a bell tower
and you the bell. As you ring,

what batters you becomes your strength.
Move back and forth into the change.
What is it like, such intensity of pain?
If the drink is bitter, turn yourself to wine.

In this uncontainable night,
be the mystery at the crossroads of your senses,
the meaning discovered there.

And if the world has ceased to hear you,
say to the silent earth: I flow.
To the rushing water, speak: I am.

- Rainer Maria Rilke, *Sonnets to Orpheus II, 29*

I wasn't sure how I would know when I had made it past the worst of things—how I would know this lonely side path was drawing closer again to the boulevard of a life that is more about living than about death.

I thought that if more of the legal issues with the estate were ironed out, I would have some peace and I could process my emotions better. I theorized that if we finalized the memorial bench his coworkers donated, and I scattered his ashes there, maybe then I would be at a threshold, a step away from the edge of the liminal space of grief.

But as things progressed and I achieved those milestones, I realized the true benchmark of "success" in my grief process would be when I was more sad than I was angry. When I actually missed him, instead of being pissed off at him. When I found something of his and felt softer inside, instead of harder.

I did reach that point, although I have moments where it's still easier to be angry. Sadness seems like an odd measure of success, for sure. I'm wise enough now to know that I get to name my successes and be proud of them, even if other people don't understand why that is a success.

Part of acknowledging success is looking back and naming what worked. For me, much like other people I've met who have made it through something awful, it wasn't about identifying that one perfect thing that was the answer. It was about throwing everything at my grief, believing that SOMETHING was bound to help, and most of all TRYING. I knew for sure that I was not going to sit around and wait for the rage to go away or cross my fingers and hope the maniacal jitters would just calm down on their own. I was definitely not going to spend the rest of my life panicking every time I saw someone napping and thinking that they were dead.

I had kids to raise and a business to run.

So, I tried everything anyone mentioned that sounded vaguely congruent with my personality and values.

Here's a quick review of the things I tried, many of which I have highlighted earlier in this book. Friends and family supported me in learning about and making time for many endeavors, which is a primary role for anyone close to a person experiencing loss.

- I went back to my old therapist whom I hadn't seen in years. It was comforting to see him, and good to know he was still there, and I could still visit the familiar office. I felt like a much older and much more weathered version of the woman who used to sit in the chair next to the box of tissues with my silly worries and complaints.
- I attended the support group for people who lost a loved one to suicide. I was dubious about it at the start. I had done lots and lots of work on myself before this happened, and I thought it would be a waste of time to sit in a circle with people who had perhaps never thought deeply about their purpose on earth or taken the time to write out their commitments to their loved ones. In fact, it didn't matter at all. We each had such a deep shared experience, and so many things to say that were very impolite to say anywhere else,

that I was incredibly grateful for every single person in that room. Besides which, anyone who has endured suicide grief has automatically pondered their purpose on earth.

The support group also had a structure, following the chapters of an Alan Wolfelt book, that was comforting and predictable. And they were so gentle. If you didn't read any of the book, it was okay. If you didn't want to talk or share, it was okay. If you took five packs of Skittles when you left, it was okay.

- I spent a few hours in a sweat lodge, the moist hot air searing my nostrils and my lungs; the strange voices bellowing unfamiliar indigenous song in my ears; the impenetrable darkness leaving my mind with nothing to hold onto. I could only be present and try to breathe.
- I worked with a personal trainer at the gym who stayed with me as I struggled to open my arms and expose my chest and belly. A trainer who understood when I just needed to smash something as hard as I could.
- I used psychedelic mushrooms with a trustworthy partner, outside in nature, and felt all my fear evaporate. I communed with unconditional love. I embodied unconditional love. I experienced myself as the source of infinite love. I saw a grid of 24 facial expressions blinking from anger to happiness and from smirks to peace. I understood the temporary nature of all things, and the enduring spirit that perpetuated beneath it all.
- I went camping alone and spoke to no one.
- I used a hypnotherapist, who spoke into the part of my mind that my conscious self could not pick apart and analyze.
- I had a personal coach who focused on performance and goals.
- I had a personal coach who focused on my confidence and self-assurance.
- I listened to live music and drank scotch on the rocks while sobbing.
- I attended a group transformational training program, even though I'd already spent a lot of time in such "large-group awareness" programs five years earlier. This new brand of

emotional awareness trainings that I tried was more experiential, and more cathartic. I could fully immerse myself in my feelings and see their beauty, their ugliness, their purity and their contradictions and hypocrisies. And most importantly, their transient nature.

During one evening of the transformational training program, our class was directed to write in our journal to someone about an unresolved issue or feeling. It was already eight months after Daniel died by the time I enrolled in the program, and I didn't think I had a lot of unresolved anger. Once I put my pen to the paper, so much fury boiled out that my pen struggled to keep up.

Here is what I wrote to Daniel, a raw, unblemished tirade that I didn't know was inside me:

> F*CK YOU for leaving me alone in that room with your dead body.
> Just me.
> Just me to figure out what to do next.
> To be responsible, to make calls, deal with the police, honor all of your f*cking requests. You were always self-centered, but it didn't have to be that way. You could have found your own joy internally. You had the tools. But it was me who paid. You got to drift off and avoid the pain and end the struggle while I got to work calling your sister and all of your friends to tell them the worst news ever. To comfort them. To absorb the shock wave of their feelings again and again, call after call. To unravel the estate and the house and all of the passwords. By myself. Because you checked out.
> You f*cking COWARD.
> When I saw your hat, I knew. When I opened the door, I knew. But it was your pale, bluish arm. That was the for sure for sure end of possibility. YOU LEFT ME. YOU LEFT ME. YOU LEFT ME. You were nice enough not to blame me.
> You gave up.
> You made me not enough.
> I wasn't enough to live for.
> You left.

> I miss you.
> I miss how predictable it was.
> How safe.
> I'm sorry I didn't love you out of it.
> I'm sorry I wasn't enough.

That anger is not inside me anymore. I left it in that journal. When I read it now, I empathize with those feelings, but they aren't mine anymore.

It was during that same program that I realized one of the biggest impacts of Daniel's death on me. It was the morning of the second day of the second session. The trainer leading our session asked us if anything was happening in our daily lives when we went home that was pertinent to the work we were doing in the session. I stood up and shared that I was about 15 hours into an argument over how a traffic signal worked.

"What?" she asked, incredulously.

"Yeah, my boyfriend and I had a disagreement about how the left turn arrows work here in North Carolina, and we're still arguing about it almost a day later," I said.

"That sounds exhausting," the trainer said.

"Yes," I agreed. "I know I'm really attached to being right. It's one of the reasons I signed up for this training."

When she asked me her next question, everything screeched to a halt.

"When was the last time you were wrong and it had a big impact on you?"

Time stopped, sounds stopped, and I stopped breathing.

"Well," I said slowly, "I was living with my partner who was very depressed and anxious. He had lost his job and he wasn't doing well. I had been spending a lot of time and energy comforting him and I needed a break. I thought it would be okay if I went away for a day and recharged my own battery. So, I went out of town with my son and we hiked. I thought it would be okay. But when I came back the next morning, he had killed himself."

As I said the words out loud, I realized that it wasn't so much that I was blaming myself for Daniel's death. It was more that my usual, run-of-the-mill perfectionism had mutated into a fear that getting something wrong would be fatal. The fear in my body made so much more sense.

Later, at a high ropes course activity that was part of the same program, I was able to separate the fear instinct originating from my body and my reptilian brain and distinguish it from true danger. As I walked along a wooden beam high in the air, held securely by a harness and a thick cable, I could thank my body for sending out the warnings, and then remind myself that I was safe, and keep moving.

That's how life is for me now.

I still have more fear messages than I used to.

But now I can say, "Hey thanks Nervous System, I understand you think there's danger. There's actually no danger, so I'm going to keep going."

And then I keep going.

Because there really isn't any danger.

I'm not scared of being left alone, because I didn't die from that.

I'm not scared of dead bodies, because I didn't die from that.

I'm not scared of sudden surprises, because I didn't die from that, either.

And if I did die, I now understand that I would have no consciousness left to process the fear or pain. There would just be nothing.

Therefore, there is literally not anything to be afraid of.

I may as well choose to live, then.

Chapter 12

It's Okay to Triumph

"Nobody will protect you from your suffering. You can't cry it away or eat it away or starve it away or walk it away or punch it away or even therapy it away. It's just there, and you have to survive it. You have to endure it. You have to live through it and love it and move on and be better for it and run as far as you can in the direction of your best and happiest dreams across the bridge that was built by your own desire to heal."

- Cheryl Strayed, *Brave Enough*

The world isn't owed our contributions or our talents. But I don't know anyone who would say prior to something bad happening, "I hope I get completely caught up in it and my life is derailed, and my life is about nothing else but this tragedy. It becomes my life story."

No. People don't wish that.

I want people to maintain all their chances to contribute their gifts to the world. I don't want the story of my life to be, "Oh my god, she's the one whose husband killed himself." I don't want the story of anyone else's life to be a tragedy either.

I want that tragic event to be in the opening scenes of a biographical film about whatever unlikely story will unfold during the remainder of our days, which we will never be able to predict. But it will be a triumphant story, in which we faced adversity and persevered, a story in which we overcame something difficult. Not a story in which something difficult overcame us.

It is common knowledge that anyone who has suffered a physical injury must face some pain and push through it to heal and get stronger. A year before Daniel died, I had traveled to New York City for work and gone for a run on Long Island. I'm a runner and tend to explore new places by running in them. On Long Island, the road surface was different from what I was used to, and as I was looking around at the trees and plants, I tripped on a crack in the road. It was one of those falls where I didn't have any sense of losing my balance and trying to catch myself. One second, I was mid-stride and the next, my knee had slammed into the pavement, and I was rolling to the side, trying to minimize an impact that had already happened.

I managed to jog back to the house where I was staying and put ice on my knee. The next day I limped through LaGuardia and got on the plane back home.

Back in Columbus, I started physical therapy to heal my knee injury. With a doctor standing over me, I was pushing heavy weight on the leg press—much heavier than I would have thought was a good idea. I did lunges and deep stretches under his watchful eye. It hurt, and I had to push through it, but I got stronger.

Today, a few years later, my knee is still not the same. It won't ever be the same. It's a little bit crooked and it sticks out in the middle in a way that my other knee doesn't. But it's strong as hell. (After the injury and the rehab, I finished an Ironman triathlon, so I know it's strong.)

With emotional injury, the average person without a clinical degree doesn't know the best treatment modality. Uneducated about the current thinking on grief processing and unmoored from normal life, people like me end up lost. Some people don't progress at all. Often, we forget that there is a time of retreat and healing, and then intentional work is required to gain strength again. Healing is a back-and-forth proposition. Time spent in restorative activity is required to provide strength for time spent grieving. Healing is not a straight line, it's a messy, liminal one. Liminality in my case means there is a pulling away from the world, a time of chaos and uncertainty and work, and a coming back together.

Although it's common knowledge that a broken leg ultimately becomes stronger at the point of the break than it was before the injury, we don't often think about our emotional strength that way.

I was taking a course recently and the instructor asked us to give ourselves a score of one to ten, indicating how strong and successful we were in each area of our life, such as finance, career, romance, fitness, and family. She told us that if we ranked ourselves above an eight in any area, we should look into that area for a major disruption, because we probably had faced serious adversity in that area of life and had emerged stronger. Adversity was identified as the SOURCE of strength and high performance!

But it's rare that we remember this truth, or that we think of the liminal journey as analogous to physical injury. If we did, we might be less likely to be pulled into an endless period of torpor and immobilization—the very thing that would render us stiff, creaky, and unable to move if we were nursing a sprained shoulder or banged up foot.

I know that the sympathy I received was pleasant, comfortable, and enabling. I could stop trying in my work, and stop making dinner for my kids, and lose track of grant applications for my nonprofit, and everyone said it was okay. I liked that place, where I had very few responsibilities. It was easy to get sucked in.

Furthermore, the sad energy that would show up in a room when I entered it was hard to resist some days. People weren't trying to bring me down, and they didn't want me to be sad forever, but their expectation that I was in a permanent state of devastation and grief made me feel like I *ought* to be a little sadder, just to meet people's expectations of being a widow. It was easy for that to become a never-ending cycle: I think people will expect me to be sad. I dress sad. I put on my sad face. I enter the meeting. Everyone sees that I look sad, and they make sad faces at me and talk to me in sad voices. Repeat.

The only way out of this cycle of sadness is to WANT out. The desire and volition to escape is helped greatly by having a strong social circle of people who can bring neutrality, empathy, and encouragement. Desire and determination were hard to access at a time when often I just didn't want things to get better. I wanted to suffer. It felt pure, somehow. I felt I deserved to suffer because I didn't support Daniel well enough. I didn't do a good enough job of showing him the beautiful and loving things in life. It felt easy when more bad things happened. It felt right that I was trying to balance both houses while carrying crushing business debt because a client had fallen way behind paying the $5,000-a-month cost for my company to employ a full-time staff member to work on his data project.

When my dream car that I had waited and waited to buy was rear-ended on the freeway and totaled, it just seemed like what was supposed to happen next.

When my life-to-date perfect dental health was suddenly marred by a weird infection that required four specialist visits and a root canal, that just seemed like destiny, or another way to prove I could sustain still more adversity.

By the time my younger son crashed two cars before his 17th birthday, including Daniel's carefully maintained "winter car" that I had inherited and given to him, it was less that I felt invincible and more that I felt numb. I couldn't imagine what else could happen, but it didn't really matter. Apparently, I was going to somehow keep trucking right through it.

Ultimately, at some point, I did break. I was driving home from Costco with a car full of groceries, contemplating bills and jaw pain, driving my son's car that was now dirty, had a broken radio, and sported bungee cords holding together the front bumper. It suddenly felt so futile. No amount of poignant Jackson Browne songs could soothe the sting. The amount of effort I was putting in just to maintain a fairly unsatisfying standard of living was too much. It was all too much, and I wanted to get off the ride. I think most people have had that thought. But the difference in being a survivor of suicide grief was that I knew exactly what it would take to end it all. I knew the right drug to buy, and approximately how to acquire it. And then there would be nothing. All the turmoil would be over, for me at least.

As soon as I started thinking that thought, I remembered what I'm so grateful for in life: responsibilities. People usually groan internally when they think about responsibilities, but for me, I've always believed that it's like Viktor Frankl wrote about the arch that holds up the building: it must have pressure on it in order to stand. An arch with no pressure will crumble. We humans are meant to have responsibilities on our shoulders. We're meant to be bearing up under stress, all the time. It's how we're designed. The people who don't have anyone counting on them are the ones who don't survive adversity. They have nothing to live for.

It took only a few milliseconds of thinking of my kids, and their approaching college journeys, and my business and its employees counting on their paychecks, to realize that dying was the dumbest idea I'd ever had.

I continued driving home, and I unloaded the groceries and paid the utility bills and scratched the dog behind the ears.

It's Okay to Triumph

***

The other things that were hard to reconcile were the benefits I accrued from Daniel's death. Not just the relief from near-constant anxiety and panic that had defined our relationship in its later years. I mean actual benefits, like six months of health insurance premiums his former employer provided. And the big house on the oversized suburban lot facing protected woods and parklands. And his retirement fund, which he had recently started funding. When he was younger, he was sure he would kill himself before retirement, so it seemed like a poor decision to fund it. In his later years, I took it as a hopeful sign that he contributed as much as he did. I knew when I read the details of what he was leaving me that, if I planned carefully, my kids could go to college and graduate with no debt.

It was challenging to know how to feel about these windfalls. It seemed positively shameful, or at least rude, to be happy about it. But truly, they were a huge relief.

I didn't want to seem ungrateful, but I found myself telling long stories about the bureaucratic difficulties in dealing with the estate. I hoped people would feel sorry for me, and that would ease the sting for them when they found out I was inheriting everything.

I had enjoyed a few days of not caring what anyone thought, right after Daniel died. I had this pure space—a clearing created by the absence of someone who always had an opinion on my choices and how I spent my time. The suicide was so shocking to people, and the consequences so grave, that no one had any right to say a word to me about anything. It didn't last long, though. It was a temporary euphoria that existed alongside the shock, guilt, and fear. Soon enough, I imagined Daniel judging me for every piece of furniture I moved, and every hole I put in the walls to hang artwork. By the time that phenomenon faded, I was back to my old habits of imagining that other people had the time and energy to judge me and were actively doing so at every turn.

Eventually I eased into a new, slightly more evolved version of myself, with more scars, less materialism, less certainty, less control, more flexibility, and a lighter step. I love myself more. I trust myself more. I know my capacity is even deeper than I thought.

Now I'm stronger. And I've made it through.
I'm more dignified. More loving.
And more alive than ever.

***

"I don't deny that there should be priests to remind men that they will one day die. I only say that…it is necessary to have another kind of priests, called poets, actually to remind men that they are not dead yet."

- G.K. Chesterton, *Punch*, vol. 242

Epilogue

Bringing Others Along

I made it, but I'm out to accomplish more than that. It feels like swinging on a rope across a canyon and making it to the other side, triumphant, but looking back across the chasm to see a crowd of people waiting.

I want everyone to make it.

I want each person to take their own path through the liminal space of grief, feel their own feelings, struggle in their own way. But I want them to make it.

The more I speak with people, the more I understand that the grieving person isn't able to learn about grief. The people I want to speak to are their friends and family members.

I'm clear that it's the GRIEVING PERSON who has the greatest impact on their growth, integration, and healing. A person who had poor mental health at the start is much more likely to have "complicated grief," which is the psychological term for getting stuck. The best family and friends in the world can't solve that. The person experiencing the loss has the most say about how they integrate the loss into their life, and how they recover. But that person very rarely can study grief or see themselves clearly in the early days. It's up to their loved ones to support them in the ways that serve them best, and they are the ones who can learn, who can change, and who can regulate our emotions and behavior around the loss.

To review, most people who encounter a sudden, tragic loss or other trauma first experience a shock stage where their survival instincts are primary, and their higher functioning is offline or at least difficult to access.

PHASE: Shock

> ACTIONS REVIEW:
> During this time, the grieving person is best served by support for their basic needs: safety, food, shelter, and sleep. If they don't feel comfortable sleeping in their usual bed because of

the loss, support them to find an alternative. Bring them hot, good-smelling food even if they say they aren't hungry. Keep them company, even if it means sitting in silence. And if they aren't sleeping, help them find support with that, starting with the mildest herbal sleep aids first and moving up if necessary, in consultation with a medical professional.

PHASE: Integration

Once the shock stage begins to wear off, the person experiencing a loss begins to move between the two "walls" of active grief in the strange passageway of this new, unfamiliar world.

One wall is Loss-Oriented grief activities and the other is Restoration-Oriented grief activities, from the diagram detailed in Chapter 7.

ACTIONS REVIEW:

As a supportive loved one, it's important to tune in to the person experiencing loss each time you encounter them, and know they are bouncing between these two types of grieving activities.

If they are actively reminiscing, feeling sad, and not wanting to do the logistical tasks required of them, they are on the Loss-Oriented side. Support that side with simple presence, calm support, and validation that whatever they are feeling is okay. Ask questions that help them settle deeper into their experience during this time when they are facing it.

If you arrive for coffee and find they are researching concert tickets, learning how to repair the house or cook meals or another role their loved one used to fill, or they don't allude to their loss at all, you will know they are on the opposite wall, attending to Restoration-Oriented grief activities. Support these by encouraging their new interests and following their lead if they are avoiding talking about the loss.

If you notice your loved one is always on one side and never on the other, that may signal a difficulty in healing.

Be aware that those experiencing a difficult loss may be resistant to the idea of "healing" and may not want to talk about healing. They have suffered a major blow, and they rightly know they will not be the same again. Remind them that serious injuries heal stronger than before, but never without a scar. They won't be the same, but they will get better.

Above all, be neutral. Being neutral creates a clear space for your loved one to grieve authentically in your presence. Being dramatic, on the other hand, with either positive or negative energy, requires the grieving person to first overcome what you are emoting to express themselves. They may also be sensitive to your experience and shy away from you if they sense the topic is too emotional for you.

When I was in the shock phase as well as the integration phase, I avoided people who reacted with high emotion to me simply because I didn't like the surprise and the drama. I'd already had enough of that. I craved calm and strength. I wanted someone I felt I could release some emotion with, and for that I wanted someone with depth, who could hold an open space for me to bring my worries, fears, rage, and shame.

PHASE: Recovery

Once the bereaved has integrated the loss, and the absence of their loved one and any associated trauma has become part of who they are and not a repeated surprise, they will move on. Seldom bouncing between the walls of actively grieving and avoiding grief, your loved one will move forward, perhaps aligning on new goals or values. Their focus will be on the future or the present, and less on the past.

ACTIONS REVIEW:
You can support the recovery phase best by not fearing new bouts of grief and integration, and by walking alongside your loved one with encouragement as they emerge, different and stronger.

You may not feel like a leader in a time of crisis for your loved one. You may actively not want to be a leader of any kind in such a situation. But if you have learned the basics of grief and appropriate support, it is your place to step up. Share what you have learned with others.

Show up confidently, move gracefully toward a person experiencing loss, and listen with an open heart.

Now you know you don't have to say or do the perfect thing.
You no longer need to be afraid.

Do not be dismayed by the brokenness in the world.
All things break.
And all things can be mended.
Not with time, as they say, but with intention.
So go.
Love intentionally, extravagantly, unconditionally.
The broken world waits in darkness for the light that is you.

- L. R. Knost, *In Humanity: Letters from the Trenches*

www.ingramcontent.com/pod-product-compliance
Lightning Source LLC
Chambersburg PA
CBHW060948050426
42337CB00052B/1877